Productive Leadership

Productive Leadership

—————————— A Guide for Ministry in the Small Church

Roy L. Spore

RESOURCE *Publications* · Eugene, Oregon

PRODUCTIVE LEADERSHIP
A Guide for Ministry in the Small Church

Resource Publications
An Imprint of Wipf and Stock Publishers
199 W. 8th Ave., Suite 3
Eugene, OR 97401

www.wipfandstock.com

PAPERBACK ISBN: 978-1-6667-1104-2
HARDCOVER ISBN: 978-1-6667-1105-9
EBOOK ISBN: 978-1-6667-1106-6

09/27/21

Contents

Introduction

I AM A SMALL church pastor. I spent forty-two years in full time service as an ordained pastor in the United Methodist Church, thirty-six of which were in town and country communities. Now in my retired years, I am continuing to serve a small, rural church. In addition to my pastoral responsibilities, through the years I have consulted with a number of churches as they have sought to do leadership training, long range planning and ministry development. I have also served as a mentor pastor to over 20 persons entering into their ministry, all of whom were serving in small churches, and I have been an instructor to persons entering ministry for three decades. During these years of service, I have learned several things about church leadership, especially as it relates to the churches I have served and the laity in those churches with whom I have been privileged to work. This book is inspired by them and is intended to lift up the things they have taught me through the years, which I am now honored to pass on to others.

They taught me that some of the most effective ministry happening in this generation is the product of creative leadership, focused on the mandate to make disciples. These leaders have seen needs within their community and found a passion for the people immersed in those needs. In response, they have created and developed some of the most incredible ministries I have seen, many of which have lasted decades, some even generations. These were ministries that emerged out of a deep and heartfelt concern for others and an intimate relationship with God, fulfilling Jesus' understanding that love of God and love of neighbor combine to fulfill the holy law. While some of these ministries have been done on a grand scale, impacting scores of people gathered in one setting, many have been small and simple, touching one life at a time. Only a handful of them have been expensive to implement; most have been done using resources of the church that were already available.

They taught me that working together is always better than working alone. I have seen deep and abiding relationships formed between people who packed summer lunches together or who worked putting up rafters on a new home. I have seen lives changed because people of the church reached out to someone in need and gave them hope. But I have also seen the givers become the receivers as they have learned the meaning of what Jesus said: "... *when you did it for the least of those among you, you did it for me.*"

They also taught me that there is a strength in small communities and the churches within those communities that both binds people together in a common cause and allows ministry to happen faster and easier than in a larger community or big church. Having served in some of those larger churches and having grown up in one, I have learned that there is an intimacy in smaller churches that is difficult, if not impossible, in larger ones. This intimacy leads to a personal connection with one another that makes them like family, facilitating dialogue and uniting them together in a common cause. Their time together extends beyond an hour or two on Sunday morning and often the best interaction takes place at the grocery store or the football stadium.

They have taught me that ministry is not the product of doctrine, but of faith, and that no single denomination or religious perspective has a monopoly on effective ministry. While my history is exclusively United Methodist, my experience in working in multi-denominational settings and cooperative ventures in ministry have enabled me to realize that there are a lot more things that unite us as the people of God than there are those that drive us apart. I have seen arguments over doctrinal differences fade away in the passion for helping others. I have seen people of the same denomination willing to set aside their differences in order to unite in ministry. I have seen churches on the verge of closing find new life as they have given birth to new ministries. Most importantly, I have seen churches suffering from deep divisions re-united by outreach ministries as they stopped focusing on themselves and turned their hearts to others. When we are faithful, God uses us in ministry, regardless of our theology, background, experience or perspective.

Above all, they taught me that when it comes to ministry, there is no greater motivating factor than a deep faith. Faith should be the heart of everything we do in the church, but often budgets, buildings and bureaucracy take precedent over the outward expressions of our beliefs. Some of the greatest ministries have been given birth in Sunday School classes and Bible studies rather than long-range planning sessions and committee meetings as faithful church members found their hearts strangely warmed in hearing the scriptures in a new way. I have also seen deep seated prejudices disappear when confronted with the truth of the Gospel, leading congregations to open their doors to persons of different ethnicities, lifestyles and economic situations, to people who had previously been shunned.

All of these teachings and more have inspired me to write this book, having found a strength and vitality in small churches that is often ignored and neglected. Many of my colleagues view the rural church as a relic of the past, a dinosaur facing extinction. In terms of membership, several United Methodist Churches in the Dallas metroplex have memberships larger than the combined membership of all the churches in the rural county that is now my home. This fact is echoed in every other mainline denomination in our area. Yet these same small churches have been a training ground for young pastors who receive one of their first assignments to a rural congregation. Armed with the latest theories from seminary and professional teachers, these pastors have discovered that not everything about ministry can be learned in a classroom and that the greatest teachers are those who have been on the frontlines of service, often for decades, riding a rollercoaster of ups and downs, suffering financial crises, listening to sermons that had yet to reach their full potential. These wonderful saints have loved, nurtured, encouraged, and persevered, knowing that someday, somewhere, this neophyte of ministry serving their church would make a significant difference. We would all do well to learn from these saints and what they have discovered about being the church and making a difference in their community for the Kingdom of God.

Therefore, this book is not about the latest theories of church development and it does not find its strength in academic research. Instead, it is based on my personal observation and experience and seeks to present what I have actually seen happening in small churches. It is also not about specific ministries, though several are mentioned, or how they might be implemented. It is about how leaders have come to work together to bring shape to God's vision in their lives. It is not about the latest management theories or corporate models and it does not prescribe a set of programs that, if implemented, will provide success. In other words, instead of beginning in books and trying to find where the principles they set forth can be observed, this work begins with seeing the ministry churches are doing and asking the question *"Why does this work?"* and *"What can we learn?"* Taking these lessons learned, I have sought to bring them forward in an organized and systematic fashion, leading to what I call *"Productive Ministry."* For me, this term emerged as I was working on my doctoral studies decades ago and seeks to focus our attention on the results of our study and ministry together rather than the activities in which the church engages. What is presented here is a progressive understanding that leads to that end by focusing on the leadership of the small, rural church.

The organization of this book focuses on two broad topics. The first seven chapters lift up the work of the church and attempt to reveal common elements in churches that are effectively engaging in productive ministry and how they were led into that ministry. Each chapter in this section deals with an aspect of developing ministry from four perspectives. First, it begins with a scriptural image that frames the reality of what I have observed. Unless otherwise noted, these passages are presented as they appear in the New Revised Standard translation of the scriptures. It then moves to an understanding of the small church that identifies some of the issues and obstacles that they face, called *"Doing Church."* In the third section of each chapter, *"Seeing Church,"* I attempt to present the issues that have been identified in a real setting, using the struggles and victories of congregations and their leaders to illustrate the principles involved. Each of these stories is factual, either from a church to which I have been appointed or from a congregation with which I have worked, though efforts have been made to protect the privacy of individuals and the churches they serve. In the final section, which I call *"A New Perspective,"* I seek to establish the truths about ministry that I have learned from the previous discussions and how it applies to the way in which the church and church leaders engage in developing ministry, setting the stage for the following chapter. At the end of each chapter in this section is a series of practical exercises in which leaders and congregations might engage, helping them to appropriate the information and ideas in their own ministry setting.

The final chapters of the book shift the focus away from the church and its outreach, toward those who lead the church. Based on my observation and experience of effective and productive church leaders, both lay and clergy, I have sought to objectify my observations by naming certain qualities of leadership and briefly exploring their meaning. After a discussion of leadership in general and how to view that leadership in a way that leads to productivity (chapter 7), I explore the different ways in which we might envision leadership, focusing on the character of productive leaders (chapter 8) and their competencies (chapter 9). Bringing the two sections together, chapter 10 explores the contributions of productive leadership, focusing its attention on the fruit that is evident through the ministry of productive leaders in productive churches. The final chapter seeks to cast a vision of the future church and how productive leadership can shape that future.

In all of these chapters are both observations and information that probably touch the experience of the reader and elicit a sense of "déjà vu." Therefore, the beauty of this book, from my perspective, does not rest in any sense of groundbreaking insight, but in the opportunity to draw connections with the reader's own experience, to learn from those experiences, then to adjust the way we do ministry in a manner that enables the church to be more productive and bear fruit for God's Kingdom. To that end, it is probably at its best when read together by leaders of the church. Therefore, I recommend that churches consider using it as a group study, to learn how to bring out the best in one another's leadership, to benefit from the experience and understanding of others, and to work together to enhance the productivity of their church's ministry.

Finally, it should be noted that while the focus of this work is on the small, rural church, the principles and truths that it points to are not exclusive to this setting for ministry. Indeed, the process of discerning a vision, the life of the church, the character of leadership, and the many other components discussed also find an important place in larger churches in different settings and may be just as effective in these settings. However, if I have learned anything at all in my ministry, it is that ministry in a rural setting is different from that in an urban or metropolitan environment. This difference may be quantitative, but it is not qualitative. Great ministry happens in both settings, but how it happens is often quite different, as are the incentives for that ministry. Therefore, this work is undertaken with great gratitude for leadership in the small church, but also with a sincere appreciation of ministry and leadership in those larger churches. And while the principles contained herein speak directly to the smaller church, leaders in larger congregations may find them beneficial in their setting as well.

Thus, I pray that each of you who take the opportunity to read and reflect on the words of these pages may find them a blessing, that God my use them to enhance and strengthen your personal leadership in the church, and that your churches may benefit from the conversation that ensues as together we seek to make disciples of Jesus Christ for the transformation of the world!

1

A Foundation for Productive Leadership

Once while Jesus was standing beside the lake of Gennesaret, and the crowd was pressing in on him to hear the word of God, he saw two boats there at the shore of the lake; the fishermen had gone out of them and were washing their nets. He got into one of the boats, the one belonging to Simon, and asked him to put out a little way from the shore. Then he sat down and taught the crowds from the boat. When he had finished speaking, he said to Simon, "Put out into the deep water and let down your nets for a catch." Simon answered, "Master, we have worked all night long but have caught nothing. Yet if you say so, I will let down the nets." When they had done this, they caught so many fish that their nets were beginning to break. So they signaled their partners in the other boat to come and help them. And they came and filled both boats, so that they began to sink.

—LUKE 5:1–7

PETER AND ANDREW HAD been fishing all night, with nothing to show for their efforts. They were undoubtedly tired from their work, perhaps frustrated from their lack of success, and possibly even questioning the future of their chosen profession. Then Jesus showed up and everything changed: the emptiness of the night's labor was transformed into a miraculous catch. In this brief story is a model for productive leadership. Consider the unwritten portions of this story.

As fishermen, Peter and Andrew were accustomed to hard work. They had invested themselves completely in a profession that was, at the very least, adequate for their livelihood and perhaps, at times, quite lucrative.

1

From their years of experience, they knew how to catch fish and they knew where to catch those fish. Their nets were woven to suit the needs of their craft. Their boat was designed with a shallow draft, as were most of the fishing boats on the lake, so that they could easily maneuver into the shallow coves where the fish gathered. They read the tides and phases of the moon to know when to fish. Their training, their understanding, their ambition, and their commitment came together to create a proven system for success. Yet on this night, that success had not come.

As they were cleaning their nets, Jesus came walking along the beach, followed by a throng of people. Did the fishermen know Jesus? Probably: they were, after all, from the same region and, according to Luke's version of the story, Jesus had healed Simon's (Peter's) mother-in-law at some point in the past. Thus, there was a high likelihood that their willingness to let Jesus use their boat was not simply an act of blind obedience. Yet the Jesus they knew was not a fisherman: he was carpenter who had recently begun itinerating throughout Galilee with a message of hope for the people, accompanied with acts of mercy toward the sick and possessed within their midst. Why, then, should they trust this itinerant preacher who acted like he knew more about fishing than they did?

His instruction to them was to, *"Put out into the deep water and let down your nets for a catch."* This suggestion went against all of Peter's understanding: his boat was better suited for the shallow waters of the shoreline; his nets were tightly woven to capture schools of fish; his training and experience were more suited for his traditional methods. In short, he was not ready for what Jesus asked him to do and he saw no future in it: *"Master, we have worked all night long but have caught nothing."* Yet something led Peter to trust Jesus: maybe it was the prophet's charismatic personality; maybe it was the miracles Peter had already seen and heard about; maybe it was nothing more than a desire to prove to Jesus that fishing is best left to fishermen. In his acceptance of Jesus' challenge, Peter found yet another miracle: his nets were filled, his success was granted, and his future was ensured.

Doing Church

Echoes of Peter resound through the contemporary Church. Countless studies of the local church in today's society bear out a profound truth: churches that were once dynamic and vital now suffer from an aging membership, decline in attendance, economic crises, and an absence of youth and children. This fact is especially true in rural areas, where churches tend to be small, community and family oriented, and very traditional. Each year scores of these churches close their doors, unable to counter the trends that bring about their decline, and even more fall into a downward spiral of hopelessness. Like Peter before them, leaders of these churches carefully clean and tend their nets, preparing to cast them yet again into waters that will not produce enough fish to sustain them. Feelings of frustration run rampant in the local church, lifelessness gives way to despair, and, eventually, even the leaders begin to disappear, questioning their sanity in giving themselves to what seems to be a hopeless cause. Yet, while this scenario seems to be the accepted norm, is it the inevitable future of these churches? Many would say "yes" to this question, citing what they believe to be the cause: a fundamental trait in smaller, rural churches, expressed in the now-trite phrase, "*But we've never done it that way before.*" There is a perception that these churches would rather die than change. Thus, while their community/neighborhood changes around them, the church seeks to remain the same, holding on tightly to the past to preserve what little they have left and guarding the traditions that they once held dear. While this is certainly true of some of the churches, it must not be taken for a general principle. The majority of churches that I have encountered would do almost anything to keep their doors open and their ministry vital. It is not that they are afraid of change: they fear that making changes will rob them of their identity and heritage, both of which have provided meaning for their lives of faith. Change is all too often presented as an "either-or" choice and church leaders are caught up in a tug-of-war between what they have been and what others think they should become. It is quite possible that the future of these churches does not depend on who wins this battle and that, in fact, even engaging in the tug-of-war at all may be a source of decline and despair. Perhaps the future of the small, rural church rests on a very basic understanding of who we are and what we are called to be. With this in mind, let us re-visit Peter's story by noting three things.

First, Peter knew what he was doing long before Jesus showed up. Peter and Andrew were not amateurs, occasionally trying their luck by dropping a net into the water; neither were they "fair weather fishermen" who only set out in their boat when the conditions were optimal. Their life depended on their success and they were in their boat, casting and hauling in their nets, day in and day out. Their experience had taught them how to be most successful and they used that experience well. The issue that they faced was not that they did not know what they were doing: they did; but in this particular moment, their old, proven tactics weren't working. In order to catch fish, they needed a new point of view, and Jesus provided that new perspective.

We make a serious mistake when we assume that the reason for the decline of the small church is that they do not know how to "do" church. Most of these churches have endured for generations; many of them have been bastions of hope and deliverance within their communities through the hardest of times. The elders of these churches were leaders long before most of the people reading this book were born. They have received, trained, and sent forth seminary students and new pastors throughout the decades, often imparting their wisdom, sharing their knowledge, and giving their love to men and women who were just beginning to explore and realize the meaning of ministry; and when professional ministers were not available, they continued the work of the church under the own leadership. In myriad ways, these churches have given more than they have received. We owe to them a huge debt of gratitude for being the church in places where, without them, there would be no guiding force within the community. Instead of dismissing their leadership as archaic and irrelevant, we should honor them as the saints, learn from them how to face hardship, and celebrate with them the many triumphs of their legacy.

As we consider the future leadership in these churches, we must do so by honoring the past leadership that is already present. The standard cry of the small church is *"We need new leaders."* It is a cry that must always be heard, for new leadership is always needed for the continuity of the church: from each new generation new leaders must be raised up to take on the mantle of responsibility. The older, veteran leaders of the church often face a sense of futility, continually casting the nets of their service into waters that produce no fish. They are tired, weary of performing tasks that seem to produce nothing, blinded to any possibilities of the future being different from the current trend. But simply raising up new leaders does not ensure the future success of the church. Someone needs to train these leaders and that responsibility falls upon the saints of the church. Jesus did not send out a new team to catch fish: he taught the existing team a new way of fishing, utilizing what Peter and Andrew already knew and redirecting it to make it productive.

Thus, the second observation is that what Jesus offered was not a fundamental change in what Peter was already doing, but it did require a new mindset. Jesus did not tell Peter that he had to go buy a new boat; he did not compel him to fashion new nets; and most importantly, he did not tell him he was wrong and that he didn't know how to fish. Furthermore, Jesus didn't suggest to Peter that the method, location, and practice of fishing to which he was accustomed was irrelevant and archaic and that he must abandon what he already knew. It would be fair to assume that, in spite of the miraculous catch, had Peter continued to fish for fish, he would still return to shallow bays and coves and the methods that had worked well for him in the past and that, in all likelihood, he would have continued to catch fish in these locations and with these methods. But Peter also would have been more willing to move into the deep water, to try out some new possibilities, knowing from his experience that a new way of fishing would also produce fish, most of which could not be caught in the shallows.

What Jesus offered Peter was a new opportunity for practicing what he did best, and that created a new vision for his future. Proverbs 29:18 declares: *Where there is no vision, the people perish* (KJV). Churches always rise to meet their vision: churches whose vision is one of hope and growth will rise to make that vision a reality; churches whose vision is of decline and demise will experience the fulfillment of this vision. Too often, the only vision that small churches have is not a vision of hope, but a vision of decline and defeat and they fail because this is all they can see before them. Leadership that produces abundance does not abandon the past but builds upon it to find a new vision for the future. Yet that vision seldom comes from within and certainly cannot be seen when the focus is on perpetuation of unproductive practices. Ministry in the local church that is productive is born out of a vision of God's Kingdom within their midst, which in turn is the result of a deep and personal relationship with Jesus Christ. Thus, productive leadership is always spiritual. Without Jesus, Peter would have continued doing what he was doing. Maybe it would have been adequate; perhaps at times it even would have been successful. But without Jesus, it would never have been miraculous. Jesus gave Peter a new vision, a new perspective, a new possibility for his future that carried the promise of an abundant catch.

Third, the obedience demonstrated by Peter, which was likely based on a prior relationship with Jesus, provided the opportunity for the miraculous catch. It was not the simple invitation of Jesus that brought about the catch, but that invitation combined with Peter's faithful response. Peter might well have declined the invitation to set out into the deep water. He certainly knew more about fishing than Jesus did. The weariness of an unproductive night's work clearly gave him justification for declining the opportunity for more work. But Peter agreed and moved into the deeper water. It is possible that Peter remembered what had happened at his home with the healing of his mother-in-law; at the very least, even if he had not witnessed them firsthand, surely Peter would have heard stories about miracles that had taken place in other homes, in other towns, in other lives. Knowing what had happened in the past created a sense of trust in the ability of Jesus to work wonders in the future.

As small churches in rural areas hear the invitation to move into uncharted territory, they must do so remembering the past and how God worked in and through them. Naming and claiming those moments of triumph from their past provides a reason to trust a new vision for the future. While a large part of this retrospective claiming will be to see how they, as the saints of the church, rose to meet the challenges before them, an even greater part is to recognize the empowerment of the Holy Spirit in the midst of those challenges. Thus, to be ever spiritual means to see that the successes of the past, whatever they might be, came about because they were willing to listen to and obey the call of God in the life of their church; knowing how that call led them in the past creates a trusting relationship that can lead them into their future.

Yet in the midst of all this comes a striking reality: it was not Peter's vision or desire that brought about the miracle, nor that of his fishing team. Only the vision brought into the moment by Jesus made possible the catch. As leaders consider the importance of finding a vision, they must realize that too often the guiding vision of the church comes from within, based on their own desires or needs. There are also times when the vision is created by seeing what others are doing or following the latest trends. While both of these are important, however, leaders must remember that the vision that brings in God's Kingdom is God's vision, and that vision can only come through careful and prayerful discernment of what God wants through the church.

It is also interesting to note that when the miracle happens, the first thing Peter does is to call his friends and partners James and John. Granted, it was motivated by the need for help, the nets being too full for Peter and Andrew to manage on their own, yet the instinct on Peter's part was to involve others in what was happening. Similarly, when the church rises to God's vision, the natural response is to invite others to join in, sharing the abundance with friends, family, partners, and colleagues, and the beneficiaries of the miracle grow as others come to share in discipleship.

Seeing Church

Within the leadership of First Church there was a genuine desire to make changes in order to attract younger families, so they contracted with a "consultant" to help them move into their future. Seeing the sanctuary for the first time, which was built during an era when preaching was the focus of worship and the pastor was elevated (literally) to a position of prominence, this consultant quickly declared that the first thing the church had to do was remodel the sanctuary, remove the pulpit and the chancel rail, and create a greater sense of openness to the worship space. His hasty recommendation was met with extreme resistance. The sanctuary had been built at a time that was still recognized as the pinnacle of success for the church, under the leadership of a pastor who was revered for decades after he left and still held a special place in the hearts and minds of many of the older leaders. Most of the current church leaders were the very same people who, in the younger years of their lives, raised the funds for that sanctuary over thirty-five years before; others were married in that space and still carried with them the memories of joy that being in that sanctuary evoked; still others celebrated the lives of their parents in that sacred space as a final act of worship at their funerals. The suggestion of that space being irrelevant to future generations may have been accurate, but the insistence on changing it was met with extreme fear and resistance. From that point forward, the consultant was viewed as an outsider who was trying to strip away everything that was sacred to the congregation and, while his directions to the congregation were often on target and might well have helped the church grow, his words fell on ears deafened by the fear of losing their identity.

A New Perspective

Much of the resistance to change encountered in smaller churches comes because implementing change implies abandoning their past. Looking back on that very negative experience five years later, the leaders of First Church realized that they held an unhealthy attitude during the consultant's visit.

They deemed him as an "outsider" and were hesitant to trust him, certain that he could not possibly identify with the congregation, their heritage, and their needs. His hastily expressed recommendations regarding the sanctuary only confirmed the prejudice that they carried. Had the consultant taken the time to learn their story and the incredible importance that the sanctuary held, he might not have made the hasty recommendations or, at least, would have couched them in terms that honored the sacredness of that space in the minds of the leaders. As a summary evaluation, the church leaders came to understand that any changes that they made must be seen in light of their heritage and bring honor to the saints of their past. This reflection would eventually pave the way for the creation of a new space in the form of a fellowship hall. The chair of the building committee was a young adult in the church when the sanctuary had been built and, very wisely, tapped into the excitement of the previous experience to fuel enthusiasm for a new space, not to replace the old, but to allow the church to extend its ministry into new waters. In this new space would be an open stage that could be used for music programs, dramas by the children's departments, and, yes, contemporary worship.

Small rural churches are not doomed to failure and death. Many of these older congregations have found a new life and a new energy for ministry by catching a glimpse of new possibilities, but that new vision is almost never imposed upon them by an outside source. In a small church, the recommendations of consultants and the strategies of judicatory emphases are generally received with skepticism and doubt. Yet when the vision emerges from within the leadership of the church, it is received in trust, especially when it reflects the heart of the congregation and members have had a voice in its emergence. If the church is to receive a new vision that compels them to set out for deeper waters, from whence will it come?

Setting Out for Deeper Waters

If the small church is to move into the future with a sense of hope, it must find that hope in a new vision that comes from God. Fishing in unproductive waters will seldom produce that hope. Leaders must be willing to make some changes in the way they do certain things. But they must also learn from the past, honoring the saints and their heritage, learning from them, and using the experiences of God's work in the past to guide them into what God will do in the future. They must place their relationship with God at the heart of everything they do and learn to trust God's leading, even if it doesn't make sense to them or goes against the status quo. Doing this brings about a sense of partnership that inevitably leads to the presence of miracles and the inclusion of others.

Growing Leadership

Take the time to think through the history of the church, especially the more recent history in which the leadership has participated. In your reflection, make note of the following.

a. When was your church founded and what circumstances led to its birth?

b. If possible, use the records of membership and attendance to chart the church's progress for the last 25 years. Note the periods of change, especially if those changes appear to be radical (major shifts in one direction or another) and seek to identify any causes for these changes.

c. What were the most memorable events that you can recall? What made them so memorable?

d. Was there a particular time in the church's history that you would call its "highpoint?" If possible, make note of the characteristics of the church and its leadership during this period of time.

e. What were the moments of crisis that the church has faced? What was the nature of this crisis and how did the church move past it?

f. Name the people that emerged through the years as the true leaders of the church and identify the characteristics of their leadership. Are there any common elements that seem to reappear in this list?

2

The Effective Church

Now the eleven disciples went to Galilee, to the mountain to which
Jesus had directed them. When they saw him, they worshiped him;
but some doubted. And Jesus came and said to them, "All authority in
heaven and on earth has been given to me. Go therefore and make disciples of all nations, baptizing them in the name of the Father and of
the Son and of the Holy Spirit, and teaching them to obey everything
that I have commanded you. And remember, I am with you always, to
the end of the age."

—MATTHEW 28:16–20

OFTEN REFERRED TO AS "*The Great Commission,*" these final words of instruction to the disciples make clear their mandate: to make new disciples.
Furthermore, the disciples they were to make were not from a single location, nor did they belong to a single group. The phrase "of all nations" implies that the mission field of the original disciples was unlimited by ethnic
origins and geographical boundaries. In other words, the entire world was
to be their mission field and every person they met would be a potential
disciple. The fulfillment of this mandate would be measured by the disciples made. Conversely, failure to make disciples would be counter to the
mandate.

The Church's mission is to make disciples: to introduce persons to the
God who loves them, lead them to walk in the path that Jesus trod, and empower them to be agents of God's grace and reconciliation. In this mission
the Church finds its identity and its purpose. All other missions must flow
from this one and any that are contrary to it are contrary to the expectations of God. But what does it mean to "make" disciples? Once again, Peter's

initial call becomes a model for us. After sharing in the miraculous catch, Peter was both amazed and humbled, realizing that he was in the presence of the Holy One. Seeing Peter's response, Jesus replied, *"Do not be afraid; from now on you will be catching people."*[1] It would take a while for Peter to learn what these words truly meant, but what he discovered was that the net he would cast was the net of God's love and the fish he would bring in were the people gathered into God's love. Who those people were and where he would find them would grow and expand as Peter and the other disciples (in Luke's gospel and the Book of Acts the author refers to these original followers of Jesus as the "Apostles," the ones "sent out") matured in their understanding of Jesus and what it meant to live in the power of the risen Christ, but the mission never changed. That same mission has been passed on to each new generation of Christians, to each new emergence of the Church, and is now the responsibility of this generation. Likewise, each new generation has had to learn how to fish in the waters around them, using the knowledge and understanding passed down to them from their forebears. How they fished, where they fished, and who they gathered in the nets was constantly changing, is still changing, and will never cease to change. The task of the current generation and each local church is to learn how to use what has been passed down to them to catch the fish in their own waters and to be brave enough to set out into the deep when necessary. Hence, each leader is called upon to fish for people and each church is called upon to produce a catch of disciples.

Doing Church

Effective ministry in the local church makes disciples. In recent years there has been a strong tendency to equate making disciples with bearing fruit, based on the many allusions found in the gospels. Lovett Weems, Distinguished Professor of Church Leadership at Wesley Theological Seminary, has written extensively on this concept and his work is worth noting here.[2]

In Matthew's version of the Sermon on the Mount, Jesus brings his words to a climax by instructing the people that the "goodness" of a tree

1. see Luke 5:10b

2. Two books are worth noting here: Weems, Lovett H. Jr. *Church Leadership*, Nashville: Abingdon Press, 2010;

and Weems, Lovett H. Jr. and Berlin, Tom. *Bearing Fruit*, Nashville: Abingdon Press, 2011.

is determined by the quality of the fruit it bears.[3] This is but one of several images that the Lord uses to invite his followers to examine their lives and the lives of others by the fruit that is produced. Indeed, this image permeates the entire narrative of the Bible, with the word "fruit" and its cognates appearing over 180 times. The strength of this image must not be taken for granted: bearing fruit is a mandate for all of God's people. In <u>Bearing Fruit,</u> the authors suggest three ways of understanding God's call to bear fruit.[4]

First, there is the fruit of God's expanding reign. Rooted deeply in the Hebrew Scriptures, God's desire is for Adam and Eve, Abraham, Moses, and the entire nation to expand the reign of God throughout the world by increasing the number of people who fall under that reign. Clearly, this is what Jesus had in mind when he instructed the Apostles to "make disciples." Bearing fruit means using the blessings God has given in order to extend the influence of God to others, that they may be included in the expanding reign of God.

Second, there is the fruit of righteousness. Living in a covenant relationship with God transforms a person, changing the bent to selfishness toward a sense of beneficence toward others. In the New Testament, this transformation occurs through a personal relationship with Jesus Christ and in that relationship the transformed person seeks to live a life of service toward others. Yet unlike the self-righteousness of obedience that comes from the following the Mosaic law, Paul clearly argues that the true transformation of a person's life can only come through grace[5] and that this new life of grace leads to a life of true righteousness after the image of Jesus. This righteousness is not seen in devotion alone, but in the actions of faithful people as they lead their lives seeking to be "Christ-like" in their relationships with others, within their families, through their chosen professions, and in the example that they set for all that see them.

Third, there is the fruit of justice. The authors define justice as " . . . *the expectation of God that all people will find adequate resources to enjoy life.*"[6] The image of the vineyard set forth in Isaiah 5, which was retold and reworked in Jesus' parable of the vineyard (Matthew 21:33–41), holds God's people accountable for the fruit they produce: having received the vineyard as a gift of grace, the expectation is that it produce a harvest pleasing to

3. Matthew 7:15–20
4. *Bearing Fruit*, pp.2–9.
5. see Romans 3:21–26
6. *Bearing Fruit*, p.7.

God, to become nourishment and bring pleasure to those around it. Using God's resources selfishly, without regard to the plight and condition of others or to the obligation to the owner of the vineyard, is displeasing to God and contrary to the mandate to bear fruit. Surely this is what Jesus had in mind when he told his followers that people are known by the fruit they bear.

In each of these three images of fruitfulness can be seen an outward thrust: bearing fruit is not to be understood as self-fulfillment, but as the fulfillment of God's desire. Furthermore, the gift of grace that brings transformation is not for the blessing of the individual, but so that the individual can become a blessing for others. Put in another way, it is not simply the character of a person or the degree of faith that is the criteria for effectiveness: the criteria for effectiveness is the fruit that is produced so that the reign of God may be extended, so that righteousness may become a way of life, and so that justice may prevail within the world. This understanding has led Weems to set forth a "so that" manner of doing ministry, which focuses not on the action of that ministry, but the purpose: ministry undertaken "*so that . . .* "[7] (more will be said about this later in the discussion of visioning).

Of course, bearing fruit assumes that the small church *wants* to fulfill the mandate set forth by Jesus to make disciples. While this may not be a foregone conclusion and there are certainly some churches that truly would like to remain exactly the same until the day that they die, these churches are few and far between. When given a viable vision for their future, the majority of churches, small or large, rural or urban, will rise to the occasion and learn how to make disciples anew. The problem isn't their desire, but the options often placed before them by their vision. As stated by Lovett Weems:

> There is a hunger for a compelling message and a commitment to an essential mission. People are weary of cures that don't cure, blessings that don't bless and solutions that don't solve.[8]

Faithful Christians want to hear and share the Good News; they want to rid themselves of the demons that might lead to their demise; they want to be involved in the greater Kingdom of God as they give of themselves to mission and ministry. But too often the desire to be in ministry and make

7. *Bearing Fruit*, p.19.
8. *Church Leadership*, p.15.

disciples is lost in leadership that is ineffective in its mission field or, sometimes, absent all together. Too little attention has been given to developing leadership within the small church. When it is available, leadership training and development has often been focused on a subsistence ministry that has little or no vision. It is sometimes focused on implementing the latest trend or seeking to duplicate the most successful movements. Too seldom does it seek to empower the church to find its own vision and shape the life of the church to meet that vision. Absent of effective leadership, churches are often left casting their nets over and over into the same waters, weary and frustrated that the fish they once caught are no longer there. They need a new perspective on making disciples and a new beginning for their fishing: they need to set out for deeper waters.

Seeing Church

First Church was located in a small community of about 3,000 residents on the edge of the county. It was an old, established congregation with a century of history. It had experienced some good times of financial stability and growth during the tenure of some beloved pastors, but most of its history was marked with tension and disagreement, usually when the pastor suggested new possibilities for ministry or when they struggled to meet financial obligations. As a result, with only two exceptions, for 125 years the average tenure of pastors at the church was less than two years. As with many congregations, in the early 1960's it reached its peak membership under the leadership of one of those beloved pastors and built a new sanctuary. It was an incredible change for this church, but one that they welcomed and that brought growth into their midst. However, in the three decades that followed, the church had experienced slow and steady decline. Nevertheless, it was a reasonably healthy church that always rose to meet whatever crises they faced, whether it was repairs for the building or tragedy within the membership.

A new pastor was appointed to the congregation who honored the traditions of the church's past yet invited them to look toward their future. In a few short years, he, too, became one of their beloved pastors and the church experienced a new vitality and some modest growth. Fueled with a new sense of energy and hopefulness, a new Sunday School class was formed for young adults. As the class began to grow, it produced new church members, most of whom had not grown up in the church. Members of this class approached the pastor with a request to start a new worship service, one which would be more appealing to their desires for worship. The request was well received and the pastor, along with the worship committee, began to work toward the creation of this new service, but when a goal of "within the next year" was set, the Sunday School class was not pleased: they wanted it now. However, the worship committee knew that the addition of a new service was not to be taken lightly, that there were many things that had to be put in place for the service to be successful, and that a six-month timeline would provide the opportunity to properly prepare the leadership and the church for this big step and to publicize the new service to the community.

Shortly thereafter, the pastor left for an extended study leave, during which time the associate was given responsibility for the ministry of the church. The new young leaders in the church seized the opportunity at hand and convinced the associate to start the new service immediately. Their argument was compelling: "We'll provide the leadership for the service; we'll pick the hymns; we'll recruit laity to help; we'll invite the people to join us; all you have to do is show up and preach." With two weeks of preparation, the new service was launched, with about 80 people in attendance, close to half of the average worship attendance in the established service. It was lay led, the music was contemporary, and, in spite of a few minor miscues in the service, it went well. The following Sunday attendance dropped to less than 60 and for the third week's service only about 40 people showed up. By this time those who had agreed to plan and lead the service had lost their enthusiasm and more responsibility was falling on the church staff, especially the associate pastor. Many of the instigators of the service had stopped attending, finding that the early time, which they claimed would be an advantage, was in fact an inconvenience when it came to helping their children get ready for church.

When the senior pastor returned from the study leave, the service was in its seventh week and attendance had dropped to under 20. It had also become a pastor-led service, after the volunteers had abdicated their responsibilities. The associate, devastated by a sense of failure, recommended discontinuing the service. This recommendation was echoed by the worship committee, who felt like its authority had been usurped. However, the pastor knew that to do so would signal defeat, to the young adults, to the church as a whole, and to the community. Instead, he recommended continuing the service, but using it to explore the meaning of worship, giving themselves permission to try new and different styles of worship while honoring the twenty or so people who found worshipping at an earlier time to be a blessing. With the support of the church staff, especially the musicians, the early service continued. After each week's worship, the staff and a few lay leaders would reflect on the service, what seemed to work, what did not work, and, especially, who was in attendance. After several weeks of experimentation and many heartfelt conversations, the service began to develop its own rhythm and routine, settling in to a very relaxed and informal time with no formal liturgy but plenty of opportunity for participation from the congregation. The music became a blend of newer worship music and older hymns sung in an upbeat manner. Little by little, attendance at the service grew and it began to attract persons from the community. After about six months, the church leadership realized that, of the people who joined the church, 75 percent had done so at this early service.

Reflecting on the experience, the church council reached a clear understanding that would shape the development of future ministries: new ideas should be encouraged to emerge, but they must be seen as a continuum of what is already present in the church. The hasty launch of this new service without the benefit of extensive preparation resulted in the young adults initially seeing themselves as emerging leaders, pioneering new ministries, but resulted in a sense of failure. On the other hand, the seasoned leaders of the church saw this new group as a threat to the establishment and wanted to take a *"See, I told you so"* stance as a way of affirming their own leadership and the values it represented. The competition that resulted could have led to a defeat for both sides, and the veterans realized that it was this approach that had led to a lot of the struggle of the church's past. Yet when a new alternative was presented, one that was not out of either perspective and did not require a win-lose solution, the church prospered, and disciples were made.

A New Perspective

How does ministry happen? In small and rural churches, and probably in others as well, ministry tends to happen in one of two ways: it is either born out of what the church wants or what the church needs. More specifically, the origins of local church ministry often rest in either the longings of the congregation or in circumstances that compel the church to take some form of action; by either desire or necessity, and sometimes by a combination of both.

Usually, new ministries are given birth in the desires of the people, which are often sought and expressed in planning meetings, prompted by the question *"What would you like to see the church do?"* Generally speaking, the answers to that question are based on conversations already taking place within the membership. They reflect the heartfelt longings of the members as they seek to find a vision for the church that addresses their personal lives or as members reflect on the desires of the surrounding community. In all these cases, the answers indicate a desire to see the church move forward, in a positive direction, in order to make it more relevant in the lives of the disciples. There have been a lot of effective and creative ministries given birth out of such desires as the church seeks to fulfill the expectations of its members and what they want to see.

Yet often the ministry of the church is shaped by the circumstances of its current moment, by pressure from outside authorities or by nothing other than the will to survive. As needs present themselves, from whatever source, the church seeks to respond to those needs in a positive way. In the best-case scenario, the response of the church is based on the depth of their understanding of the scriptures and reflects what they perceive to be the will of God, rooted in the values of the church. However, often the response to needs is based on how to meet those needs in the quickest, least painful manner without compromising the values of the church and has little to do with seeking to fulfill the mandate of God: emergency funds are raised to pay bills with no thought to the meaning of stewardship; roofs are repaired with little thought about the souls that will sit beneath them; a nursery is created because Aunt Susie has to bring her granddaughter to church with her, but no one considers reaching out to the mother who is struggling to make ends meet as a single parent.

Ministry happens somewhere on the continuum between desire and necessity as these two motivating factors are held in tension. Ministries driven by desire may be said to be proactive, reaching forward to shape the life of the church around the desires of its members; ministries that grow out of needs are reactive, developed as the church responds to its present situation. Effective small churches have learned how to work out of the tension created by these two poles, blending the two in order to address both the needs of the church and the longings of the congregation. Thus, effective ministries emerge as the church seeks a balance between the needs they encounter and the desires and longings of the people, as they face the emerging needs of their facilities, their lives, their community and their world, balancing the expectations of the people with the values of the institution.

Needs of the church:	MINISTRY	Desires of the People
Reactive		Proactive
Institutional		Personal
Based on Values		Based on expectations

The tension created between these two poles provides the opportunity for the church to be in ministry and can lead to effective programs and activities. However, there is another possibility: if not balanced, the probability is that ministry becomes either a self-indulgent exercise in narcissistic pursuits or an attempt to preserve the past. Moving too far toward the desires of the people, a proactive approach toward ministry focuses too narrowly on fulfilling those desires to the exclusion of the needs and values of the church. It can become quite selfish and territorial, leading to jealousies and self-promotion. On the other hand, a reactive approach to ministry that moves too far toward the needs of the church becomes an attempt to preserve the values and history of the institution to the neglect of the people and their expectations. It can become a cold and lifeless attempt to maintain the status quo as the church lives too much in the past and ignores the changing world around them. Both of these are common problems in smaller churches. Thus, while the upside, positive outcome of balancing this tension is effective ministry that uses the values and heritage of the institution to fulfill the desires and longings of the congregation, the downside, negative result of an imbalance results in a dysfunctional congregation that either ignores their values and chases after their whims, or one that staunchly seeks to maintain the status quo of the past at all costs. The upside makes new disciples; the downside does not.

Setting Out for Deeper Waters

If the small rural church is to move forward in effective ministry, it must learn to live in the tension created between the needs of the church and the desires of the people and use this tension to grow and develop so that it can make disciples. At the same time, it must find its vision and strive to live up to that vision. But the vision it finds cannot be based exclusively on either of the two poles; it must come from another source. Albert Einstein is attributed with the saying: *"Insanity is doing the same thing over and over and expecting different results."* Without a new vision, ministry can easily become an exercise in fishing the same waters over and over and thinking that, someday, the fish will return. Effective ministry moves out of the shallows and dares to fish in the deeper waters. Effective ministry may emerge out of self-fulfillment and attempts to provide a continuity of the status quo; it also may derive from taking care of emerging needs, both within the life of the church and within the community. But the new vision required to make disciples is the product of a desire to bear fruit for the Kingdom of God. Thus, the future of the church may depend on effective ministry becoming productive, focusing on producing the fruits of the Kingdom and making disciples. Productive ministry requires an intentionality that looks to the future of God's reign and its focus is on producing disciples for that Kingdom.

Growing Leadership

a. Make a list of the values of your church as you perceive them. These may take the form of guiding principles that are used in decision making or they may be rooted in the traditions of the church.

b. Look back at the history of the church developed earlier. What factor did the values of the church have in shaping the traditions of the church? What influence did they have in the turning points? Are these values shared by the majority of the congregation?

c. Make a list of what you consider to be the longings of the congregation. These may be expressed in conversations, or they may simply be perceptions of their desires. You may also couch this response in terms of *"What are the expectations of the church members?"*

d. Consider the current ministries of the church: have they derived from the expectations of the people or the values of the church?

e. To what extent does your church seek to preserve its status quo? Would you consider this a positive attribute of your congregation?

f. How sensitive is your congregation to the needs of your community? Does it regularly seek ways to reach out to its neighborhood?

3

Becoming Productive

That same day Jesus went out of the house and sat beside the sea. Such great crowds gathered around him that he got into a boat and sat there, while the whole crowd stood on the beach. And he told them many things in parables, saying: "Listen! A sower went out to sow. And as he sowed, some seeds fell on the path, and the birds came and ate them up. Other seeds fell on rocky ground, where they did not have much soil, and they sprang up quickly, since they had no depth of soil. But when the sun rose, they were scorched; and since they had no root, they withered away. Other seeds fell among thorns, and the thorns grew up and choked them. Other seeds fell on good soil and brought forth grain, some a hundredfold, some sixty, some thirty. Let anyone with ears listen!"

—MATTHEW 13:1–9

How DOES THE CHURCH,[1] and how do churches, bring in a catch that effectively produces disciples, bearing fruit for the Kingdom of God? Perhaps the key to this understanding rests in what it means to be productive. There are several definitions of the word productive that inform this discussion. The first three of those found in Dictionary.com are: [2]

> 1) having the power of producing; generative; creative
>
> 2) producing readily or abundantly; fertile:

---

1. In this work, Church (with a capital "C") refers to the universal Church, while church (lower case "c") refers to the local church.

2. "*Productive*," Dictionary.com, © 2019 Dictionary.com, LLC.

3) causing; bringing about

In these definitions, three words stand out: creative, fertile, and causing. Perhaps a fitting image for these definitions can be drawn from Jesus' parable of the sower and the seed. In his explanation of this parable[3] Jesus helps his disciples understand that he is (and later they are) the sower, that the seed is the Word of God, and the soil is those who would hear that Word. The abundant harvest comes when God's seed is sown on fertile ground. Drawing from this image, we may postulate that a productive ministry is evidenced by a harvest that comes as a result of the efforts of disciples to plant the Word into hearts and minds willing and ready to receive that Word; once planted, then God brings the growth. From this image then, come three principles of productive ministry.

First, productive ministry is given birth out of God's Word. At the heart of all productive ministry is a passion for the Word of God that leads to an intense search of the scriptures and results in a deep understanding of the will of God. This passion leads to an intimate relationship with the risen Christ wherein individuals and churches yearn to live in the example of the one they seek to follow. The intimacy of this relationship results from a desire to know and love God, not as a casual acquaintance, but as a trusted partner and friend. Thus, searching the scriptures does not mean a casual review of what the Bible says, but a thorough investigation of the gospel story in a manner that allows it to be a true guiding principle. In this sense, "God's Word" must be understood in the larger sense of its meaning, as set forth in the opening lines of John's gospel: *"In the beginning was the Word, and the Word was with God, and the Word was God."*[4] The search of that Word is not merely an effort or desire to know the words of the Bible, but a determination to comprehend and assimilate the essence of the message that it brings to all humanity and to apply it to one's contemporary setting. As this understanding emerges, so does a desire to share the message of hope and reconciliation with others, which is the basic understanding of "evangelism." Evangelism, in turn, is the primary activity of making new disciples. It is also the basic principle in helping persons grow in their discipleship.

Second, the work of the church is to be responsible in planting God's Word in fertile soil. Clearly evidenced in a productive ministry is a love of

3. Matthew 13:18–23

4 John 1:1

others and a desire to include others in the Kingdom of God. This principle assumes more than a basic knowledge of the context of the ministry taking place, understood as the community of the local church: it assumes a connection with that context. Therefore, inherent in a productive ministry is both a knowledge of the local community and a love for the people who live in it. In this sense, the local community is akin to the waters in which Peter fished, with which he was intimately familiar. In the modern vernacular, this principle is often expressed as *"knowing one's mission field."* Yet, at the same time, productive ministry is open to the deep water, the people beyond the immediate and traditional outreach of the church, so it is constantly aware of the possibilities of extending the love of God beyond its immediate mission field as well. While this might mean expanding that field geographically, for smaller churches in rural areas this most often means being willing to see in their midst the people who are unseen. All of this is in search of the fertile soil that longs for the Word to be planted in their midst.

Third, since the harvest is brought about by God, productive ministry is characterized by an innate confidence in God's ability to bring the necessary growth. In this sense, productive ministry must be seen as a partnership between the leaders of the church and God. This partnership, along with the other two basic principles of productive ministry, forms the basis for this chapter and the following exploration of productive ministry.

Doing Church

Ministry is given birth in the tension between the desires of the people and the needs of the church. For decades churches have approached the development of their programs out of this tension as they have sought to bring a balance between the expectations of the congregation and the values of the church. Each of these two poles merits further explanation.

No one comes to the church by accident: everyone comes with a sense of expectation. This expectation takes on many forms: a desire for community; the fulfillment of one's faith; the alleviation of some form of suffering; curiosity about what the church offers; fulfillment of a sense of obligation. The extent to which the church fulfills these expectations is the determining factor in a church's growth: when people find the church meeting their expectations, they find a place where they can belong. Likewise, when the expectations of the existing members are met, they are more likely to be involved in what the church is doing. Thus, the presumption here is that if a church is able to meet the expectations of the current members, it will be healthy, and if it can meet the expectations of the surrounding community, it will grow. While this conclusion is true to a point, it has a flaw: what happens if the expectations of the people are self-serving? What happens if the church compromises its values in order to accommodate the community? What happens if the expectations of the people are contrary to the teachings of the scriptures? Focusing the ministry of the church on the expectations of the people may, indeed, promote growth and stability, but it does not always make disciples. Thus, ministry that is effective and productive must pay attention to the expectations of the people without totally compromising the values of the church, lest the church become a club to which people belong rather than an agent for love, grace, and transformation in the world.

In similar fashion, the church must know and honor its values, thus bringing a sense of institutional stability to the congregation. But what happens if those values honor the institution without regard for the needs of the people? What if those values are focused on the maintenance of the building to the exclusion of outreach? What if the values of the congregation open the doors of the church to the people in the community who are like-minded, but close them to people who are different? Once again, the flaws of extremism quickly lead to an institution that is stable, but stagnant, to a church that may be revered within the minds of the people, but which fails to honor the risen Christ.

Therefore, effective ministry emerges only out of a healthy balance between the desires and expectations of the people and the values of the institution. Keeping these extremes in tension requires the church to maintain a healthy dialogue between the two. Churches that seek such an effective ministry must create a process that allows for the expression of the expectations of the congregation as well as the perceived needs of the community, while also identifying and honoring the values of the church. Approaching ministry in this manner enables the church to honor both sides of the tension, utilizing its strengths to address the needs expressed and discerned regardless of the beginning point or process. Effective ministry emerges out of the healthy balance of this tension, maintained by seeking a compromise between the two poles. However, there are two weaknesses inherent in this model.

First, it is based on compromise, defined as *"an agreement or a settlement of a dispute that is reached by each side making concessions."* [5] Compromise is reached by increasing the strength of one pole while decreasing the strength of the other in an effort to maintain a balance of the tension. Compromise is a highly effective means of maintaining harmony within the church because it is a viable solution to conflict, but it requires a great amount of give-and-take. To reach balance, ministries of the church are shaped by finding a way to honor and appreciate both poles, but when conflict arises decisions must be made about the extent to which one side or the other receives that honor. How are these decisions to be made? If the needs of the church are in conflict with the values of the church, either the values must be compromised, or the needs must go unmet. Compromise may bring harmony but reaching that compromise may be a barrier to the development of effective ministry. How many churches have closed because reaching out to a changing community required compromising their values?

Second, when placed in the context of our initial image, this polar model for ministry leads the church to continue fishing in the same waters. Taken in this sense, the development of ministry may be seen as an inductive/deductive challenge. An inductive approach to ministry looks at the needs of others and seeks answers within the values of the church; a deductive approach looks at the values of the church and decides if they could, or should, meet the needs. But what if the values themselves are inadequate for meeting the needs? Using the same values over and over, the church becomes like Peter casting his net repeatedly into waters from which the fish have departed. Any effort toward compromise, therefore, only seeks to maintain the balance of what already exists, ignoring the possibilities of what might be. Productive ministry seldom emerges out of compromise. In order to move toward productive ministry, the church needs to consider a new approach. A collaborative approach to ministry seeks to move beyond the current realities of the church, using them to shape a future possibility, thereby working around the pitfalls of compromise.

Seeing Church

Meeting to develop its plan of ministry for the next five years, the church council began its work by engaging in an in-depth study of its neighborhood.

5. *Oxford Dictionaries*© Oxford University Press.

Once the most prominent church in town, as well as one of the largest, the veteran leaders of the church had envisioned themselves as the elite within the community and took pride in the grandeur of their building, designed by one of the region's top church architects and complete with custom stain glass windows. To maintain this image, upkeep of the property took precedence over all other expenditures in the church, often to the neglect of its outreach ministry. The current leadership, as had been the case in the past, was dominated by professional people, some of whom were natives of the city, some of whom had moved there because of the opportunities available within the community. Realizing that effective ministry must seek to meet the needs of the people, they began their work by studying up-to-date demographic information in order to determine those needs. What they discovered shocked them initially, then spurred them to re-think their priorities.

The community that had existed when the building was completed had changed over the five decades of its life, as had the social status of the membership. The affluence of the near downtown area of this town and country community had moved outward, leaving property in the once elite neighborhood to decline in value. From the upper-class professionals that once inhabited the area surrounding the church, the demographics now indicated that the neighborhood was populated by families from the lower economic class. Surveying the distribution of the current members in terms of their residence, the leaders discovered that well over half of them lived more than a mile from the church. They also discovered that the average annual income of the church members had declined in recent years, indicating a shift in economic possibilities. Clearly, the assumptions about the church, it's mission field, and it's available resources were based on the memories of the past rather than the realities of the present. With this new insight and encouraged by the pastor and staff, the conversation about future ministries of the church moved from *"What can we do for the church?"* to *"What can we do for our community?"* and possibilities for new ministries began erupting like popcorn. Much of the discussion focused on strengthening ministries in which the church was already involved, including the support of local food pantries and financial assistance to persons in need, calling for a greater awareness of the good these ministries did within the neighborhood. Some of the discussion focused on dreams that were well outside of their five-year window of strategizing and were put in a "someday in the future" category. Yet when the day was done, a short list of goals that were possible in the near future was agreed upon and included providing space for a summer program that would help at-risk children with their reading skills during the summer months, a minor re-model of a janitor's closet to include a washer and dryer that would be available to the homeless, a back-to-school fair that the church would host to provide school supplies and resources for the neighborhood children, and opening the church building periodically so that homeless persons could use the showers, which had been built in a new addition to the church twenty years earlier but were seldom used. Implementation of these and several other outreach ministries was scheduled in a stair-step fashion over the five-year future under consideration. While there was a fair amount of vocal opposition from some of the longtime members of the church, by-and-large the congregation found a new energy in these plans, as well as some new opportunities for personal involvement.

Without realizing what had happened, in this planning session the church council had moved from competition to collaboration. Instead of seeing the maintenance of the building and its beautiful space as an established value that was in competition with the needs of a changing neighborhood, the members of the council began to reflect on how that very same space could be used to address the newly perceived needs of the surrounding community. What emerged from the reflection was a totally new thrust for the ministries of the church that moved their focus away from themselves and toward those in need.

A New Perspective

The time has come to consider a different approach to doing ministry. Rather than seeking to manage conflict created by the opposing poles of ministry, there is another approach that reaches beyond the peacekeeping of compromise: collaboration–*"the action of working with someone to produce or create something."* [6] As a remedy for conflict, collaboration seeks to preserve the best of both sides of the tension without compromising either. Thus, a collaborative approach to ministry would honor both poles, using the strength of each to reach a solution that exists beyond either. The word *"synergy"* may also be used to describe this approach, seeking to create a new possibility out of the relationship that is greater than the sum of the two parts. The answer to the question, *"How do we make disciples?"* may not

6. *Oxford Dictionaries,* © Oxford University Press.

be found in either meeting the needs of the people or maintaining the values of the church, but in a collaborative effort that moves past the current possibilities of either. Instead of each of the two poles pulling in opposite directions, a collaborative approach to ministry draws out of each of the poles to create something new. In many ways, this is like Peter taking the skills he already knows and moving out into deeper water for his catch.

In developing new ministries, the church may begin with the identification of its values, then explore how the core values of the church can address the needs of the people and community. Developing ministry in this way may be seen as a deductive approach to ministry: beginning with what is already established and deducing the possibilities inferred. However, developing ministries may also emerge by first exploring the needs and expectations of the people and community then seeking to find ways to meet those expectations out of the established values of the church. This approach may be considered to be inductive. In education, deductive learning begins with what is known then moves to discover what may be further understood; inductive learning begins with what needs to be known and moves toward what can be perceived from the current knowledge base. Likewise, a deductive approach to ministry leads the church from what is already existent within the institution, expressed by its values and traditions, to what future possibilities might emerge; an inductive approach to ministry begins with the expressions of need or expectation from within the congregation and community and decides what can be done to meet those needs and expectations out of the existing strength of the church. A collaborative approach to ministry seeks to honor both of these two poles yet seeks a solution to the conflict that may lie outside either. The result is a resolution to the conflicting poles that does not seek to maintain the tension but uses the best strengths of each of the poles to move in a new direction in ministry. Instead of the word "collaboration," Mary Parker Follet speaks of this process as "integration." Writing in 1924, she said:

> *The truth does not lie between the two sides. We must ever be on our guard against sham reconciliation. Each must persist until a way is found by which neither is absorbed, but by which both can*

contribute to the solution. Integration might be considered a qualitative adjustment. Compromise a quantitative one.[7]

As this manuscript is being prepared, there is a commercial running on television for a popular beverage. The tag line in this ad is: *"The question isn't whether your glass is half-full or half-empty; it's 'how are you going to fill your glass?'"* The same statement may be made of ministry in the church: the question is not whether we should use an inductive or deductive approach, whether we should begin with the needs of the people or the values of the church; it's *"How are we going to produce disciples?"* The truly effective church moves away from the goal of harmony through management of the tension and toward collaboration as the best source of developing ministries that make disciples. Rather than emerging through either a deductive or inductive approach, each of which is rooted in existing values, traditions, needs, and expectations, ministry that is effective and fruitful focuses its attention on the goal of that ministry. Instead of seeking to maintain and address what is, fruitful ministry dares to look at what might be. Its focus is on the fruit the ministry produces: it is a productive ministry.

Setting Out for Deeper Waters

Developing productive ministry invites leaders to address three key questions. First and foremost, they must look to their mission and ask: *"What are we trying to accomplish?"* The answer to this question arises out of the vision of the church and not only dominates all that is considered but becomes a constant source of inspiration and drive for the dialogue from which the ministry will emerge (see chapter 4). The second question is *"What must we accomplish?"* Here the needs of the people are recognized and placed in the context of the vision, expressed as expectations. Finally, the leaders must ask: *"What needs to be preserved, and how can it be used to accomplish our mission?"* In these three questions is the formula for moving beyond competition and compromise toward a collaborative process that not only provides the means for the fulfillment of the mission but also produces harmony within the congregation and fruit within the mission field.

7. Follet. *Creative Experience. pp.156, 162, 163.*

Growing Leadership

a. Using only your current knowledge, create an image of the community surrounding your church. Describe the people in that community in terms of income, education, lifestyle, etc. What do you think these people need the most? What do they expect from the church?

b. Using one of the many demographic tools available (see "Additional Resources" in the bibliography), create an image of your community based on the same criteria set forth above.

c. Compare the two images you have created. How accurate is the image created out of your personal knowledge? What can you learn about your perceptions of the people in your community?

d. Using the list of values created earlier, compare the expectations of the community with the values of the church. Where is the potential conflict? What can be done to manage that conflict?

e. What would you like to see happen in the lives of the people in your community? What resources does the church have that can make this happen?

4

Finding the Vision

About noon the next day, as they were on their journey and approaching the city, Peter went up on the roof to pray. He became hungry and wanted something to eat; and while it was being prepared, he fell into a trance. He saw the heaven opened and something like a large sheet coming down, being lowered to the ground by its four corners. In it were all kinds of four-footed creatures and reptiles and birds of the air. Then he heard a voice saying, "Get up, Peter; kill and eat." But Peter said, "By no means, Lord; for I have never eaten anything that is profane or unclean." The voice said to him again, a second time, "What God has made clean, you must not call profane." This happened three times, and the thing was suddenly taken up to heaven.

—ACTS 10:9–16

AS THE EARLY CHURCH began to emerge, Peter and the apostles struggled to find their place within the world and to understand the real mission to which God had called them. Since they were descended from Abraham and they had come to understand that Jesus was, indeed, the expected Messiah, they assumed that their mission was to the Jewish people and that they were to convince those people that Jesus was the Christ, the one who had come to renew and restore the nation Israel. Furthermore, they had heard Jesus tell them that their ministry was to begin in Jerusalem and, while in the Temple, they had experienced the miraculous arrival of the Holy Spirit. All of this put together convinced them that, out of the nation Israel, God would raise up a new people, who would become the ones gathered for God's new purpose, the *ecclesia*, the Church. Then, when in Joppa, Peter received a vision that would change everything he understood about his mission. In the vision, he saw those animals which, in the kosher laws of the Hebrew people, were not to be eaten because they were deemed "unclean," yet he was invited to eat of them. The message of the vision was: *"What God has made clean, you must not call profane."* The meaning of these words and the purpose of the vision would become clear as he was invited to the home of Cornelius, a Roman centurion, a gentile deemed unclean in the prejudices of the Jewish people: Peter was to move past the pre-conceived notions that separated him from those who were different, overcome the barriers that hindered him, and engage in a relationship with which he was terribly uncomfortable. Once again, Peter was being invited into deeper waters in order to fulfill the purpose set forth by God; and once again Peter would witness a miracle. In obedience to the invitation God had given him, when Peter met with Cornelius and his family, he saw that God was already at work in their lives and that they, too, received the Holy Spirit. In those moments, perhaps Peter recalled what he himself had said on the day of Pentecost as he quoted the prophet Joel:

'In the last days it will be, God declares,
   that I will pour out my Spirit upon all flesh,
      and your sons and your daughters shall prophesy,
   and your young men shall see visions,
      and your old men shall dream dreams.

Acts 2:17

What is a vision? It is an image of a future reality, an image of what has yet to emerge and unfold in the life of an individual, group, church, nation, etc. When the word "hope" is added, it is a vision of a *preferred* reality. But, sometimes, the vision of hope calls the recipient into a life that, at least initially, is contrary to the status quo and may even appear to be abhorrent to current standards. This was certainly the case with Peter's vision. It is safe to say that Peter's vision came as an unexpected shock to his value system and standard of behavior that had always been his lifestyle, yet on the other side of that vision was a blessing from God that would change Peter's life. The Hebrew scriptures are filled with resplendent stories of people receiving visions of hope. While these stories vary in the mode through which God communicates, they also have common features, some of which we can see in Peter's vision.

First and foremost, those visions come from God and guide the recipient to what God wants them to see, know, do, and understand. Peter's vision called him beyond the reality of his own world, shaped by centuries of customs and practices that the Hebrew people adopted out of their understanding of the Law. He was invited to see, instead, God's world, shaped, not by obedience to standards of behavior, but by God's universal love for humanity. The tension between the values held by Peter and the needs of the world, represented by Cornelius, was shattered by a new perspective on the tension with which Peter had made his peace: he was quite comfortable living his life as an obedient Jew who had come to follow Jesus and let the gentiles meet their destined fate, whatever that was to be. His world and the world of the gentiles were separated by centuries of custom and he had no reason to bring the two together. Having received this vision, however, Peter was compelled to reshape his thinking into a new image of what the Kingdom of God looked like. When God's vision comes, whether to a church, a community or to individuals, it is generally earth-shaking and requires radical change.

Therefore, as a second point, we must understand that a true vision of hope is not *our* image of a preferred reality, but *God's* image of that reality. Our image of hope is shaped by what we long for. It comes from the deep desires of our lives as we anticipate our future. But as the Apostle Paul reminds us,

> *For now we see in a mirror, dimly, but then we will see face to face. Now I know only in part; then I will know fully, even as I have been fully known.*
>
> *I Corinthians 13:12*

Regardless of the scope, ambition and loftiness of *our* vision, it still comes from the imperfection of our desires. The true vision of the Kingdom of God can only come from God and that vision is of God's future reality, not our own. That is not to say that we have no role in visioning, but that whatever vision emerges must be inspired by and seen in the light of God's work. Thus, the Church must not seek its own vision but that of God. We must not find our own vision and seek God's blessings on it, but find what God is already doing in the world and seek to join it. When Peter finally met Cornelius, he discovered that God was already at work!

Third, although the story is of a single moment when God's vision appears, in the larger context of the Book of Acts we know that Peter had been wrestling with this issue for quite some time. The Apostles were caught up in a struggle to know exactly what was expected of them. What had begun as a small movement with a handful of followers rapidly expanded to encompass persons outside their expectations. Even Paul, the persecutor of the new Christians, was brought into their presence as a new apostle. Their world was changing around them and would change even more in the months and years to come. God's vision came to Peter, not to introduce a whole new concept to him, but to resolve and shape the tension already present, from which God's purpose would be their guiding force. Thus, God's vision comes to the church in the midst of struggles, to define the real needs of the Kingdom and to clarify the possibilities present in the lives of disciples. It often appears as a new direction, but it honors the faithfulness of those to whom it comes. In other words, as with Peter's initial invitation to discipleship, God's vision invites the church to use what it has to move in a new direction for the fulfillment of the Kingdom.

Finally, the vision is affirmed, either by others who share in the vision or by events that unfold. The veracity of the vision Peter received was confirmed in two ways. First it was shared by Cornelius himself through a similar vision of what was to transpire. Singular visions are rare; more often God raises a vision in the minds and hearts of multiple people in order to affirm that it is true and correct. Therefore, we must understand that God's vision is a shared vision. Second, Peter's vision was confirmed in what transpired. Perhaps Peter was skeptical of the vision when he received it, but whatever doubts he had disappeared in the evidence of what God was already doing. The Church comes to trust God's vision because they come to see God at work through it. Put simply, when we dare to live out God's visions, we share in God's blessings and those blessings affirm God's vision, in which we share.

Doing Church

Where does a church's vision originate? As noted in the previous chapter, often it is given birth in the tension between the church's values and the needs of the people. That means that sometimes it is born out of seeing the needs of the people in the surrounding community and determining what the church can do to meet those needs. This may happen in a formal setting where those needs are identified, or through informal conversation among groups within the congregation. Crises in the neighborhood or the congregation can also prompt an awareness of those needs. This vision may emerge from a single individual, who finds a passion for meeting the needs of a particular group of persons, or from a gathering within the church that sees a need and feels the church is led to meet that need. Such a need-based vision can be very compelling and effective and may even move the church into great ministries, but it can also be somewhat impulsive and lead to ministries that are underdeveloped and lack the drive to sustain themselves.

At other times a church's vision is born in the desires and needs of the church. A typical question asked in planning and visioning meetings is *"What will the church look like in the future?"* As people, presumably the leaders of the church, share and discuss their personal answers to this question a common sense of vision will emerge. Usually, this vision is summarized with a short phrase: *"A place of belonging"* or *"A church open to all"* or some similar words. This is an important step in the visioning process and reflects the heart-felt desires of the leadership. Unfortunately, meetings that focus intently on shaping this vision typically emerge out of a sense of desperation, when the leaders of the church feel compelled to address a particular need within the church. A common scenario is: *Our offerings have been declining steadily over the last several years; if we don't do something we'll have to cutback severely; let's have a stewardship campaign.* Such visions may address a particular, immediate need within the church, but also can be self-serving.

Most often, however, a church's vision emerges out of the dialogue between the two poles as the leaders consider both the needs of the church and its community and the resources available to meet those needs. Planning sessions, strategy meetings and even the routine management of ministries often seek to balance these two poles in the search for effective ministry. Therefore, a healthy visioning process may be found as the church engages routinely in a process of self-assessment. One such process that is currently being used by churches has been borrowed from the secular world: *SWOT* analysis. In this process the church leaders begin by identifying the church's *Strengths*, which can be seen as naming the resources available for ministry. Next, they move to identify their *Weaknesses*, the areas where the leaders feel they need to strengthen those resources, whether they be physical, personal or capital. Shifting their focus, the next step turns attention to *Opportunities*, which can be seen as identifying the needs and desires of the church and/or the surrounding community. Finally, the leaders seek to identify the *Threats*, those situations, circumstances and, sometimes, people that represent a barrier to the future vision of the church. By reflecting on this information, the leaders may strategize how the strengths of the church may be used to move into the opportunities, bolstering the weaknesses and managing the threats. With greater specificity in the analysis comes greater detail in the vision, leading to a stronger sense of purpose.

A similar process is used by Ken Callahan and addressed in his book Twelve Keys to an Effective Church. In this work he identifies twelve areas of focus that appear in healthy churches engaged in effective ministry and invites leaders to view each of the areas through leading questions and rate their church on their effectiveness in this area. They are then invited to use this information to identify the greater strengths of the church and how those strengths can be used to address the lesser strengths and improve their effectiveness. Using this process, many churches have succeeded in moving toward effective ministry.[1]

Utilizing these or other planning strategies can lead to a healthy balance of needs and resources, a balance that is necessary for a healthy church. Yet there is a factor that should also be consider in the visioning process that is often not seen in the discussion of needs and resources. Visions generally center around either the question, "*What do we want to do?*" or "*What needs should we be addressing?*" As discussed earlier, these questions are designed to maintain balance, addressing needs without threatening the status quo, and often lead to the perpetuation of existing values. Ministry that is productive dares to ask an even more important question: "*What does God want us to do?*" This question leads the church beyond itself, shifting the focus away from its own needs and desires, sometimes even beyond its own values, away from its own community, and toward the greater community of God's Kingdom. Asking the question can be risky, making the existing values of the church vulnerable to transformation and reshaping the people's self-image; but casting our nets into the deep water always involves this sense of risk.

Seeing Church

It was an old church in a county seat town, what many would classify as a "mid-sized" church of around 600 members. The beautiful stone building

---

1. Callahan, *Twelve Keys to an Effective Church. I strongly recommend this book and the process it sets forth, having used it frequently in my own churches and workshops that I have led.*

had been constructed in the early 1900's at a time when the city was growing, and it reflected the prosperity and prominence of its members. Located
in the heart of downtown, it was centrally located and many of the families
walked to church from the nearby neighborhood. The church became a
symbol of everything that was good in this community and the elaborate
sanctuary hosted prominent weddings, funerals, and other celebrations. By
all standards, it was a healthy and effective church.

As the decades passed, however, the community began to change
around this bastion of faith. As the downtown area grew, especially in the
years following World War II, the affluent neighborhood surrounding the
church began to disappear, replaced by office buildings and businesses. A
new highway shifted commerce from the downtown area to a new shop-
ping center and new homes began to spring up around that area. The once
prosperous railroad that fueled the economy began to decline and they
eventually closed the shops where many of the blue-collar workers were
employed. Though quite stable economically, the size of the congregation
began to diminish. The building was now totally land-locked on all sides
and the only parking available was on-street. Without realizing what was
happening, the church had doomed itself to a no-growth mode since anyone desiring to visit the church could not find a parking place. Attempts
to buy property adjacent to the church were unsuccessful, so constructing
a parking lot was out of the question. Unwilling to abandon the edifice
that was so dear to them, the leaders of the church resigned themselves to
perpetual decline as the members aged, knowing that one day the church
would simply fade into the past. This became their vision of the future.

In the glory days of the church, it had been a proving ground for tal-
ented pastors and the church was proud to have empowered so many great
leaders, but as the church began to live into its vision of decline, their pastors became older and, while great at caring for the membership, had little
interest in reshaping the vision of the church. Then, after twenty-five years
of decline, a new, young pastor came to the church in the hopes of attract-
ing young families to the aging congregation. His lifestyle was outside of
the norm for the members of the congregation and his personal preference
for worship was more energetic and alive than the traditions in which the
members had been raised and which they found meaningful. Yet he had a
pastor's heart and quickly fell in love with the members of his congregation,
endearing himself to them by extending love, care, and attention without
forcing them into change.

Unlike most who had served the church in recent years, this new pastor saw his ministry to the community as well as to the members of the church and realized that there was a large portion of the city to the south, mostly new homes and businesses, that was not being served by his or any other church. Conversations made it clear, though, that the church was unwilling to relocate and abandon the building that they loved. A new vision of ministry would have to emerge, but the pastor knew that it had to be their vision, not his. Being a strong preacher, he utilized his Sunday sermons to explore a deep question: *"What does God expect the church to be?"* Using the narrative of the Bible, he encouraged the congregation to see how God worked through faithful people to bring about God's purpose in the world, changing lives and changing hearts. Slowly, but surely, a new vision began to emerge.

The new vision focused on how the members of the congregation could introduce persons in the southern part of the city to the love of God. But practical wisdom told the leaders that they could not expect young families to come to their downtown church: the church would have to go to them. Eventually the decision was made to use the ample resources of the congregation to construct an activity center on the city's south side. Not only would this provide a space to gather young families—built as a multi-purpose facility with a large, open room and a kitchen—it would provide a great space for the existing, older members to have family reunions and celebrate special events, space that was not available in the downtown structure. What developed after construction was an intriguing model of outreach ministry: an older, stable congregation creating a mission space in a new neighborhood for young families. Used for educational and rec-reational programs initially, within the first year of operation the exten-sion ministry created a worship service that became a point of attraction and, after five years a dedicated worship space was built that included an attractive and compelling youth center. Operating on two campuses, the congregation worshiped in a contemporary "Praise and Worship" style at the extension site and maintained a traditional style at the downtown loca-tion and each of the services grew in size. Informal opportunities for learn-ing and fellowship were held at the extension center, but most weddings and funerals took place in the formal setting of the older sanctuary. Most importantly, however, the total membership grew significantly each year as new disciples were brought into the church. This old congregation that had resigned itself to a slow death found new life in a new vision.

A New Perspective

Caught up in what seemed to be the plight of so many smaller congregations in stagnant communities, this story easily could have turned out differently. Torn between the need to grow and the desire to maintain its traditional values, the leaders of the congregation could see no opportunity for a compromise between the two that would be acceptable. Based on the alternatives they had, they became content to satisfy the needs of the existing congregation as they faced their inevitable end. It was the only vision they could see. Yet when they were invited to see their church from a new perspective, the need for compromise diminished and collaboration emerged as a new possibility, the result being a ministry that moved to an entirely new model of making disciples. This vision did not come from within the congregation, that is, its established values and perceptions: it came from a deep consideration of the needs of God's Kingdom and God's desire for the church; this consideration came through hearing the message of the scriptures from a new perspective, daring to ask the question *"What does God want us to do?"* Accepting this story as one model of what productive ministry may look like and the process they undertook as a paradigm for developing ministry, there are several things that we can learn.

First, led by their pastor, the congregation changed its perspective from themselves and their current situation toward the Kingdom of God. Without this shift in focus, the church was resigned to continue doing ministry the way they had done for decades, knowing that the results it produced would never restore the congregation to its former vitality. Their story is echoed in myriad smaller congregations that are caught in a declining community, that cannot find the way to break the traditions that are so deeply rooted in and cherished by the members. Any search for a compromise between the need to gain new members and the desire to maintain their values leads to conflict that can either result in a decision to do nothing or creates an untenable situation in which the congregation is divided. The vision that they found would lead them past seeking a compromise and toward a collaborative effort to make disciples in a new way. It was not *their* vision, produced by their own values and needs, but *God's* vision, found because they sought it. If congregations expect to grow in ministry, they have to trust God enough to step outside of their comfort zone and examine their values in a critical way.

Therefore, second, their vision was the product of intense searching and it emerged over time. Too often churches expect God's vision to come in an instant insight, a flash of lightning across the sky that makes God's will and purpose crystal clear. While such an insight is possible, it is highly unlikely. Visions emerge when people seek a vision. Just like Peter's vision came in the midst of his agony over which direction the Church should go, a local church finds its vision when it is willing to study the needs of the community, be honest about the values and strengths of the church, and allow themselves to be vulnerable before God in seeking real answers to the question *"What does God want us to do?"* In the above example, their vision came into view over months, and even years, of struggle with their situation as they worked to hear and understand the mandate of the scriptures and sought to apply it to their unique situation. This intensive search was also accompanied by a prolonged season of prayer, during which time the leaders of the church asked for discernment of their vision.

Growing the ministries of the church requires commitment. We cannot expect to sit down around a table for an hour and leave with a clear and comprehensive vision of what God wants the church to be and do. Pastors must be willing to search the scriptures and discern a message for their congregations that is clear and focused and that lifts up God's call to be in ministry. Leaders must be committed to joining the pastor in studying the scriptures and must unite together in honesty and spirituality. Congregations must be willing to hear this message and use it to discern their own understanding of the role they can play in making disciples. This takes time, effort, energy, and perseverance. Too many churches lack a sense of vision because they do not seek it, unwilling to put forth the effort or unable to know how to proceed.

Finally, the vision the church discovered was not handed to them from the pastor, who promoted his ideas and garnered support from the members. It emerged from consensus as the pastor and congregation worked together. While it is quite clear that without the leadership of the pastor the vision never would have emerged, it is also clear that the vision emerged because the congregation opened their ears to hear a new message and their hearts to receive that vision. The correctness of the vision was affirmed in both its compelling nature and its wide acceptance and was a shared experience. Just as Cornelius shared the vision with Peter and became a partner in its efficacy, the affirmation of the church's vision was seen in its appeal and acceptance by the congregation.

Setting Out for Deeper Waters

Finding God's vision is a long and sometimes tedious process that requires, among other things, commitment of the pastor and leaders, patience of the congregation, spiritual awareness, and, above all, trust of God. It is discovered over time and it is affirmed in its compelling nature. But the emergence of the vision is not the final step. Once the vision begins to emerge, it must be refined and scrutinized. Simply moving into deeper waters is not enough: even there, Peter and Andrew had to go to work in order to catch the fish.

Growing Leadership

a. Using the information accumulated at the end of chapter 3, engage the leadership of the church in a SWOT analysis:

- What are the identifiable strengths of the church?

- What weaknesses are evident?

- What are the opportunities the church has for ministries within the community, based on the identified needs?

- What threats might be encountered if the church moved to address the identified needs and how might those threats be lessened?

b. Engage in a sustained (more than a single session) Bible study, whose purpose is to understand how God has worked within the church and what God expects from faithful disciples. In this study, seek to answer some basic questions in each session:

- What is the image of God represented or disclosed in this passage?

- What is the nature of humanity presented, including the revelation of sinfulness?

- How is this human sinfulness overcome?

- What is the relationship to which humanity is called in this passage?

- How does this story relate to our personal human condition and what can we learn from it?

- In what sense is the nature of our local church reflected in this passage and to what may God be calling us?

This study may focus attention on a single book from the Bible, including any of the four gospels or the writings of Paul. It may also be shaped by particular topics that relate to your church or community and represent a search for how this topic is dealt with in the scriptures. In undertaking this study, however, it is important to allow the participants to struggle with the texts and form their own understanding. While existing studies (either written or in video format) might be helpful in shaping the study, care must be taken to address the issues as they are specifically related to the church's understanding of their ministry.

5

Shaping the Vision

Then he told this parable: "A man had a fig tree planted in his vineyard; and he came looking for fruit on it and found none. So he said to the gardener, 'See here! For three years I have come looking for fruit on this fig tree, and still I find none. Cut it down! Why should it be wasting the soil?' He replied, 'Sir, let it alone for one more year, until I dig around it and put manure on it. If it bears fruit next year, well and good; but if not, you can cut it down.'"

—LUKE 13:6–9

FIG TREES WERE COMMON in the region of Judea, especially in the fertile soil of Galilee from which Jesus came, and were a staple of fresh nutrition. Not only were they found in groves for commercial production, they were also found in small gardens planted by individual families and even in the wild. However, wild fig trees seldom grew larger than a shrub and their fruit was often aborted, the roots of the trees struggling to wick moisture from the rocky soil. When properly cared for, however, fig trees could grow as large as twenty feet tall, their broad leaves providing dense shade from the summer sun. The fruit of the cultivated fig tree came bi-annually, in the early spring and in the late fall, providing both "first fruits" and "late harvest," coinciding with the Jewish festivals of Shavuot and Sukkot, respectively. The early fruit was actually formed in the winter months from the old growth of the tree, while the late fruit came exclusively on the new branches. Mature and productive fig trees, therefore, required constant tending and their mature fruit was evidence of a caring and attentive gardener. For this reason, throughout the Hebrew Scriptures the fig tree was used as a metaphor for

Israel, the leaders of the nation cast as the gardener. Jesus echoed this image in this brief parable.

While this parable is clearly used to speak of accountability and judgment, for our purposes, we need to focus our attention on the work of the gardener, who both wisely and with evidence of concern implores the owner not to be hasty in the judgment of its worth. In his knowledge of the tree and its possibilities, he knows that, with proper care, the tree can and will be productive, but that care must be given over time. Indeed, proper tending of the tree in the winter months, the time when most trees are dormant and little care is needed, will produce an abundant harvest in the spring. From this parable, then, come some valuable lessons about the work of the church and the vision that guides its ministry.

Visions are not of what is, but of what might be. While the owner of the tree saw what was, the gardener saw what could be. Likewise, the vision of the church looks beyond the present reality to see the future possibilities. While that present moment of time may look bleak, it is with a hopeful attitude that the church is willing to see the future as a place of promise. As the gardener asked the owner for his trust, so the church must be willing to trust God that from the barrenness of the moment the proper vision may yield an abundance of fruit.

Visions take time. The gardener knew that for the tree to produce luscious figs it had to be cared for in the months of the winter, not just prior to the time of harvest. With this in mind, he did not ask the owner to give him a few weeks or even a few months, but a whole year: one complete cycle of the tree's growth. Likewise, visions emerge over time. They grow slowly in the hearts and minds of the pastor and congregation as the people of the church open themselves to God's leading. During the season of cultivation, there is little evidence that the fruit is growing at all, but it is not the fruit itself that is being nourished: it is the branch that will support that fruit, either the old growth of prior years in the winter months, or the new growth of the current season for the fall harvest. The time during which the church seeks God's vision may not focus on the vision at all, but on the health of the church and its ability to sustain itself in the cold days of winter in anticipation of the new fruit of the spring. In other words, visions emerge out of a prolonged season of work toward that vision, during which the church nurtures itself toward health.

Visions must be nurtured. God does not impose a vision on the church. Left to itself, the fig tree might have attempted to bear fruit, but, due to

43

the lack of nourishment in the rocky soil, it could not sustain the growth of the fruit. Only by being fertilized could the tree produce fruit that was acceptable. Only with the planned and strategic attention of the gardener could the tree reach its potential. Churches find their vision only when they decide they want a vision, then dedicate themselves to the work necessary to let God's vision enter into their lives.

Visions require faith. Luscious fruit would come only after the gardener tended the tree over time, providing the nourishment it needed, heaping fertilizer around its base, and waiting for the results. He had no guarantee that fruit would come, since he could not see into the future, but he had the experience of the past and the knowledge of his craft, both of which assured him that doing the right things now would bring the desired results in the time to come. Visions bring the hope of new possibilities, but those possibilities come from God: people cultivate and nurture, but God brings the growth. For a church to move toward the fulfillment of their vision, they must have faith that God will bring a harvest of fruit. But faith is not passive; it is anticipatory. True faith in God's ability lives in the now moments of life as if the possibilities of the future had already arrived. A hopeful, faithful church actively lives into its vision, working toward its actualization even in the winter of its life.

Visions produce fruit. Peter's vision was confirmed in seeing the Spirit at work in Cornelius' life; the gardener's vision would be confirmed in seeing the figs hanging from the tree. The end results of God's vision, given to the church, is seen in the disciples that are made for God's kingdom, leading to the transformation of the world.

Doing Church

As stated previously, every church has a vision. Indeed, every church does have an image of what it will be like in the future, but that image is not always real, neither is it always healthy. Such visions usually emerge from the need to maintain balance and a sense of harmony within the congregation and do little to engage God's desires in their image. They have been born in and nurtured through the needs and desires of the leaders of the church. Unrealistic, unhealthy visions fall into three categories.

Some visions are hopeful, but unattainable. Like a wild fig tree growing on rocky ground, they lack the proper care and nourishment required to bear fruit. These are visions born out of a passion, usually for a need within the community, but sometimes focused on the needs of the church itself. They often relate to a lofty goal: a significant increase in worship attendance; bringing a certain number of youth into their fellowship; establishing a food pantry that will feed "X" number of families. However, if the church does not accurately assess the resources available for fulfilling this vision, it is destined for failure. Increasing worship attendance requires an invitational attitude on the part of the congregation, but if they don't invite people, nothing will happen; building up a youth program requires committed volunteers, but if no one picks up the responsibility, there is no youth program; in order to set up a food pantry, the church needs to have available space, volunteers, and a financial commitment, but if these are not present, success is elusive. For the vision to produce fruit the church needs to ensure that the resources are either available or attainable before committing themselves to it. Not only are these visions ineffective, they are also unhealthy; when a church fails to meet a vision, a pall of defeat is cast over the members and, even though the vision may have been hopeful, its failure leads to despair.

While it is true that God can work miracles and that God truly does raise up committed persons to fulfill the church's mission, even a vision well-rooted in God's desires fails if the congregation does not have the commitment necessary to bring it to fruition. It is not enough for a church to establish their vision; they must be willing to work toward its fulfillment. It falls upon the leadership of the church to do three things. First, church leaders must be realistic in establishing their vision, setting forth a strategy for its attainment that includes what resources are available, what resources need to be secured, and how the church will acquire the resources necessary. These resources will certainly include finances, but they should also take into consideration the physical space that may be needed and how that space should be prepared, the personnel needed and how they will be recruited and trained, and the leadership required and how they will be held accountable. Second, they must keep the vision in front of the people, a process often called "vision casting." Like a runner focused on the finish line, the church must direct its attention toward the fulfillment of the vision, the fruit that will be produced through it, as the completion of their calling. Effective leadership invites the congregation to share the vision by reminding them that this is the fruit God is calling them to bear and helps them live into the vision by seeing the progress made toward its fulfillment. Third, the leadership must celebrate the work done toward the fulfillment of the vision, including milestones along the journey, significant developments and people who are giving themselves to the vision.

Some visions are attainable, but not very hopeful. These are visions that do not engage the commitment of the congregation because they do not bear significant fruit for the Kingdom. They are like the fig tree growing in the family garden, which is quite healthy and well cared for, but produces only a hand full of fruit for a few people. Often these visions come from the passion of a small group, or even a single person, who works with great commitment, but whose efforts simply do not make a big impact. At other times, these visions may be owned by the entire congregation, but may not be engaging, requiring little effort or commitment for their fulfillment outside the normal activity and ministry of the church. Many of these visions are expressed in terms of "continuing a ministry of . . . " or "strengthening our ministry to . . . " These are, in fact, hardly visions at all, for they do not lead the congregation toward new discipleship. While the church may be proud of fulfilling its vision through reaching its goal, it may also, at the same time, be turned inward, doing little for the greater Kingdom of God.

While visions should certainly include goals to be met, there is a clear difference between the two: a goal is a tool for measuring progress; a vision is an image of what will result after the goal has been reached. Too often churches confuse goal setting with visioning, focusing on the measurable results of their ministry, but failing to see the difference it will make in the lives of the people. A healthy ministry includes both. Therefore, as leaders discern and establish God's vision for their church, they must ask the question *"What difference will this make for the Kingdom of God?"*

A helpful perspective on the relationship between goals and vision is set forth in Bearing Fruit, expressed in terms of a "so that" ministry.[1] The authors point to a commonly held myth in making their case: Henry Ford invented the assembly line and made cars affordable to the average family. In fact, just the opposite is true: Henry Ford set out to provide affordable cars and found that the assembly line was one tool that would help him attain his vision. As churches plan ministry, they should focus their attention on the results that it will produce by adding the words " . . . so that . . . " to their description: *"We will add contemporary hymns to our worship service . . . so that worship will be a welcoming experience to those outside the congregation."* Adopting this perspective throughout the planning process leads the church to see the effect and the effectiveness of their ministry and

---

1. Weems and Berlin, *Bearing Fruit*, 2011. *(See chapter 3, pp. 19–34)*

can become a criterion for its evaluation. Aligning the *"so that"* with their understanding of God's desire for the church enables the church's ministry to come into harmony with the mandate to bear fruit for the kingdom of God. The same holds true of finding their vision. *"First church is a place of belonging so that persons estranged from faith may experience the saving Grace of God."* Viewed in this way, both the vision of the church and the shape of its ministry are focused on the hopefulness of God's kingdom coming into their midst.

The final category of unhealthy visions lifts up those visions that are neither hopeful nor attainable. Unfortunately, the most typical vision in the small church is an image in which the church remains the same. Sometimes this vision seeks to resurrect qualities and values of the church from the past in an effort to revitalize the congregation and restore it to a former state of healthiness, but most often it is nothing more than a desire to avoid change. This vision is seldom expressed as a formal statement placed before the congregation and it is not the product of critical discernment of the church's future. It is the resignation of the members and leaders of the congregation as they encounter a sense of hopelessness in their current situation. It can be heard in the words of the members as they talk about their church: *"We're an older church that stands on traditional values"*; *"We like things just the way they are"*; *"Our church will be here until the last member dies."* That this is an unhealthy vision of the church goes without saying. While churches that hold such visions may provide some sense of meaning and comfort to those already in the congregation, they do little or nothing to make new disciples and have little or no effect on the greater kingdom of God. They are the antithesis of a productive church. Yet these churches have produced a visible legacy: one can drive down the highway and see them in every community, their doors locked, and windows boarded over.

From an understanding of unhealthy visions, then, comes a clear criterion for healthy visions: they are both hopeful and attainable, bringing together the strengths of the church and the compassion of its members. Healthy visions are, therefore, lived out in the lives of the people and bear fruit for the Kingdom.

Seeing Church

As the new pastor arrived at the church, he began to review the materials passed on to him by his predecessor and noticed a phrase that was repeated on all the official correspondence of the church: *Gather Grow Go*. His assumption was that this was a mission statement, and he was pleased to see that the leaders had moved to create this identity for the programs of the church. In the first few weeks of his tenure, he met with various leaders of the church and, at some point during each conversation, made mention of this statement and how pleased he was to see it. However, he was a bit perplexed to note that many of the leaders referred to it as their *vision* statement. Continued conversations led this new pastor to investigate a bit further and to seek out both its origins and how it was perceived by the congregation. He learned that the statement was produced by a task force appointed by the former pastor, whose assignment was to develop a vision statement for the church. Having come up with these three words, they presented it to the church council and, subsequently, to the entire congregation and it was approved.

At his first meeting of the church council, the new pastor asked the leaders to talk about this vision statement and they were both pleased and proud to do so. They explained that the idea came from a book that the pastor had read, in which the author lifted up the importance of a church having a vision statement and the task force felt that these three words captured the essence of who they were: they *gathered* as the church; the *grew* together as Christians; and the were invited to *go* into the world. Having adopted the statement, the former pastor worked diligently to keep it before the congregation, printing it on their stationery and envelopes, making sure that it appeared on all their publicity, and often referring to it from the pulpit. The entire church was proud that they had taken this step forward. The new pastor then asked another question: *"What is the church doing to live into this vision?"* This question was met with awkward silence until one of the senior leaders said, *"We don't have to live into it, its who we are."* It was at this point that the pastor realized he had some work to do and let those words linger until a deeper conversation was possible.

What had become evident to the new pastor was that, as energetic as the church was in developing a vision, they had failed to understand what that task actually meant. Their enthusiasm had led them to focus their attention on what the church *was* not what the church *could be*. So, in coming up with their vision statement, they had described how they saw themselves in the present moment. Furthermore, the statement itself did not describe a vision but a mission; it was not what the church longed to be, but what they sought to do. The result, therefore, was a catchy phrase that sounded good and created a nice, positive image, but did little to shape the life of the church and nothing to actually guide them in their ministry.

Over the coming months and even years, the pastor took the opportunity to teach the leaders the difference between a mission statement and a vision and sought to foster within them a sense of what the church could aspire to in the future. He also helped them understand that, in order for a mission statement to be effective, it should be applied to the existing and future ministry of the church. With this in mind, as new ministry possibilities arose, they were scrutinized against what was now regarded as a mission statement by asking a simple question: *"How will this ministry help us gather, grow and go?"* While some of the church leaders, who were fiercely loyal to the previous pastor and had shared in the task force that created the statement, took offense at the new pastor calling into question the work that had been done, as a whole the council found a new way to approach ministry, one that was clear and focused on what they wanted to do.

A New Perspective

The literature on church growth is rife with the importance of a church establishing a healthy vision. Virtually every book written on the subject addresses the need for a vision as both a goal toward which the church may move and a means through which it may shape its future ministry. Having a vision, especially one developed in dialogue with their understanding of God's mandate to make disciples, creates a present and future identity for the church as an institution and the members of the congregation as the people of God. Yes, it is vital that this vision become a part of the culture of the church as the leaders continually cast it before the congregation, but a vision is more than a catch phrase or a marketing slogan: it is and must be the very core of the ecclesia, the people gathered to live out their faith in worship and service. It is both the hope of the church and its judgment: the image of what it shall become, by the grace of God, and the standard by which its future is measured. And while it certainly reflects the essence of what the church *is*, it also projects what the church seeks *to become*, having a quality of *already, but not yet."*

Therefore, a healthy and productive vision moves forward from the status quo toward future possibilities. It must proceed from the values of the church, utilizing the best of what the church is in order to shape what the church might become. At the same time, it must hold those values up for examination and recognize the need for change in order for the future to be the expression of what the church has been and the promise of what it is yet to become. Perhaps the words of the Letter to the Hebrews have a meaning here: "*Now faith is the assurance of things hoped for, the conviction of things not seen.*"[2]

There is a prayer often heard in the worship of black churches that captures the spirit of what a true vision is.

> *Lord, we're not what we want to be,*
> *We're not what we need to be,*
> *We're not what we're going to be,*
> *But thank God Almighty,*
> *We're not what we used to be.*

In these words is the essence of a healthy vision: a recognition of who we are, a desire to be more, a trust of God for the future and a willingness to leave the past behind. Against this backdrop, Lovett Weems presents ten characteristics of a vision that are worth noting.[3]

1. *A vision is related to mission, but different.* A mission is what we exist to do; a vision is what God is calling us to be.

2. *A vision is unique.* While many vision statements may sound similar, each church has its own unique vision that expresses its identity and projects that identity into the future of its own setting.

3. *A vision focuses on the future.* While it both honors and grows out of the past, its focus is not on what is or what once was, but on what needs to be and what can be.

4. *A vision is for others.* It is not about growing the institution but affecting the lives of people and meeting their needs.

5. *A vision is realistic.* It takes into consideration the people who will work to make the vision a reality and the resources available to set goals that have a reasonable possibility of being met.

6. *A vision is lofty.* While realistic, a vision also stretches the possibilities for all those involved, setting a high standard that invites people to become more than what they already are.

---

2. Hebrews 11:1
3. Weems. *Church Leadership.* pp.41-45.

7. *A vision is inviting.* It should be compelling and attractive, providing an incentive for people to become involved in its fulfillment, inspiring them to greater service and commitment.

8. *A vision is a group vision.* It is not the product of one person, nor the collection of individual ideas from a group, but a commonly held image in which the people are invested.

9. *A vision is good news and bad news.* It admits the shortcomings of the past and holds the church accountable but moves into the future with promise.

10. *A vision is a sign of hope.* It dares to say, *"Look what's possible."* As such, it gives people an image of a future reality that is better than the past.

In shaping its vision, the leaders of the church would do well to take these ten points into consideration, using them to test their vision and to guide them in its expression. Yet there is another aspect of a healthy vision that must be considered: God's purpose for the church.

As leaders work to discern the church's vision, they must be willing to subordinate their own desires and longings to those of their divine calling. As set forth previously, productive ministry is a collaboration between the values of the church and the needs of the community and world, informed and shaped by the church's understanding of God's call and claim upon them. The ministry that results from this collaboration is the mission of the church, which honors the values, yet moves into the uncertainty of the future in faith. Drawing both its strength and its resources from the existing reality of the church, the leaders strive to shape what the future of the church may come to be. But a vision cannot be imposed: it must emerge over time as the congregation seeks to understand itself, its traditions, its resources, and its value in light of what God is calling the congregation to be and to do. Guided by this sense of vision, then, the mission of the church becomes more than what they are called to do; it becomes their reason for existence, around which everything in the church revolves. In moving toward their vision and the resulting mission, church leaders would do well to ask four vital questions.

What is God seeking to accomplish through our church? Answering this question invites the church to hear God's call in its life. It requires a sense of boldness on the part of the leaders, a willingness to anticipate that the answer may lead them away from some of their established norms of behavior and may even challenge their faith. The only way to find the answer is through diligent and sustained examination of the scriptures, searched in dialogue with the faith of the individual leaders and members of the congregation, and with an openness to the sense of newness that God might bring.

What can we do that would serve God's purpose? This question invites leaders to think beyond what the church *is* and to consider what the church *does*. Having discerned God's call, leaders are compelled to place that call within their own context by examining the needs of their own community and claiming the various ways in which those needs can be met. It allows them to consider future possibilities as well as current ministries and leads them to dream dreams and see visions.

What are the values held by our congregation that will enable us to accomplish this? Leaders are asked to identify the strengths of the congregation and how those strengths can be utilized to bring about new ministry, including its resources, needs, abilities and passions. It seeks to bring forward the best of the church in order to shape its ministry, to honor the past while moving to claim the future. It moves to create a dialogue between what the church honors, who it is and what it is called to become.

When accomplished, what will the church look like? The answer to this question gives shape to the vision. It allows the church to name the vision that is emerging, seeing itself in the future as that which God has called it to be. In keeping with Weems' characteristics (above), it should be specific and unique to the church in its current setting, lofty in its scope, and both compelling and engaging. It should be shared by the congregation and fill them with hopefulness. Above all, it should empower the congregation to step forth in the confidence of God's blessings and the assurance of God's guidance.

As the leaders of the church ask and answer these questions, they place their search for a vision in the midst of a multi-faceted dialogue that includes the values and traditions of the church, the needs of the congregation and community, and their understanding of God's purpose for and claim on their lives, all done within the context of their faith—an innate trust that God will empower them to rise to meet the challenges of discipleship before them. The church is the tree, rooted firmly in the soil of their community, seeking to grow where it has been planted; the fertilizer is the values and resources of the church that can bring nourishment and new life; the vision that emerges from the dialogue is the faith of the gardener who sees the potential for the future. Brought together in faithfulness, all of the elements are present, providing the opportunity for growth that comes through the holy mystery of God's grace. Then, in the new spring of their life, the seasoned branches of the tree bring forth new fruit for the Kingdom.

Setting Out for Deeper Waters

The church's vision shapes its future, giving it both a present and a future identity, as well as a reason to exist. Properly nourished, understood and cast before the congregation, it gives rise to the mission of the church, thrusting the congregation forth in ministry to the world and for the kingdom of God. The leaders of the church, through faith and faithfulness, give shape to the vision by critically examining God's call in light of their values, resources, desires, and abilities and creating a dialogue that allows the best of all these to emerge. The smaller, rural church is especially suited to carry out this process, but they often do not see themselves as having the ability or the expertise and their vision is often shaped by the difficulties of the moment rather than the hopefulness of the Kingdom, leading them to become like the landowner, who can only see an unproductive tree destined to die.

Growing Leadership

While the desire for a vision may come from various sources, the vision itself emerges from an understanding of the scriptures as the leaders of the church search for God's call upon their lives. While virtually any passage has the potential to give shape to this understanding, there are a few that seem particularly apropos. These include:

- Matthew 25:1–13; 14–30; 31–46—These three parables form the capstone to Jesus' teachings and any (or all) of the three invite the church to consider the nature of its mission and God's call

- I Corinthians 13—In this chapter Paul gives a clear definition of the nature and purpose of love. Attention should be given to vs. 4–7

- Romans 12:9–21—This passage defines the nature of Christian behavior, often called *The Marks of a true Christian.*

- John 15:1–17—The image of the vine and branches helps define the importance of the church finding their grounding and their source of spiritual nourishment in a deep and abiding relationship with Jesus.

- Matthew 18:23–35—In this parable, Jesus invites his followers to view their own behavior toward others in light of the fullness of God's grace.

- Luke 14:7–14—This parable and the related teaching helps the reader to understand the nature of hospitality and how people who are different should be treated.

- Luke 16:19–31—While containing a presage of the resurrection, this story lifts up the ethical treatment of the poor in the church's midst.

Any of these passages may be suitable for reflection as the leaders of the church seek to discern God's vision for their ministry. Each may stand alone as a one-time study, or they may be grouped together for a broader perspective. For a sustained and prolonged study, the leaders might want to look at an entire book, such as Paul's letter to the Romans or Ephesians, or the Book of James. In engaging the leaders and/or congregation in a study such as this, it is important to lead the participants to their own understanding of the passage, engaging them directly in what it seeks to proclaim. For the purposes of discerning the church's vision, there are significant questions that must be addressed:

- *What is the nature of discipleship revealed in this passage?*

- *When disciples are faithful to this revelation, what is the outcome that God brings?*

- *What is the fruit born for the Kingdom?*

- *If our church lived out the meaning of this passage, what would it look like?*

- *What ministries are, or might be, implied in the nature of discipleship revealed here?*

- *If we chose to do this as a church, what resources do we have available that would prove helpful?*

- *What would have to change?*

- *What fruit would we bear?*

Brought into dialogue with the research and reflection from the previous chapters, a study of this nature allows the leaders to see their church and its ministry in light of God's calling and should lead to a clearer understanding of their vision. Therefore, it might be helpful at the end of each study to summarize the work with a mission/vision statement: *God is calling* _____ *church to* _____ *so that it can become* _____. Moving toward a more general vision for the church, individual statements may be combined and condensed looking for common elements. Once developed, this statement should be scrutinized using the characteristics of a vision set forth by Lovett Weems and noted above.

(A flow chart for discovering the church's vision may be found in Appendix A)

6

The Advantage of Being Small

Awe came upon everyone, because many wonders and signs were being
done by the apostles. All who believed were together and had all things
in common; they would sell their possessions and goods and distribute
the proceeds to all, as any had need. Day by day, as they spent much
time together in the temple, they broke bread at home and ate their
food with glad and generous hearts, praising God and having the good-
will of all the people. And day by day the Lord added to their number
those who were being saved.

—ACTS 2:43–47

IN THESE BRIEF WORDS, Luke describes the birth of the Church and its early
routines. Following the miraculous outpouring of the Holy Spirit on the
day of Pentecost, the now new believers found themselves in virgin territory, having no precedent regarding the shape, attitude or even purpose
of their gathering together. They clearly knew that they were moving away
from the norms that had guided their lives for centuries, norms defined
by their understanding of the Jewish Law, but they had no idea of that toward which they were moving, what their lives would become as followers
of the risen Christ. What they did have, however, was an understanding
that God had brought them together with both blessing and challenge: the
blessing of a new sense of connection with Jesus, through the power of the
Holy Spirit; the challenge of sharing this good news with others. They also
understood that their connection with Jesus united them with one another
and it was out of this sense of unity that the Church would be born as they
came to understand themselves as the *ecclesia*, the gathering of the people,

summoned by God. The Church that emerged over the following weeks was characterized by several distinct elements.

First, the Temple was the focal point of their understanding. After all, it was in the Temple that the Holy Spirit had come, at a time when masses of Jewish people from the known world had gathered to celebrate the festival of Pentecost, or Shavuot as it was properly known in the Jewish language. Timed to coincide with the first (or late spring) harvest, this festival celebrated the giving of the Torah or Law to the Hebrew people as their guide toward holiness, which united them with God. The outpouring of the Holy Spirit on that fateful day signaled to Peter and the apostles that God was gifting them with another means of holiness, brought by the death and resurrection of Jesus. Returning to the Temple frequently, perhaps daily, enabled the Apostles and subsequently the new believers to recall and reclaim that experience and its meaning for their lives. Being in the Temple was a hopeful act through which they anticipated the power of the Holy Spirit coming upon them again.

But being in the Temple had an added benefit. The Temple was, in essence, the place where the community came together, not only to worship God through the presentation of their sacrifices, but to share their lives, catch up on the latest news, and learn from one another: this had been the function of the Temple since the time that it was built. This function provided the opportunity for the new Christians, as they would come to be called, to converse with others, tell their stories, and persuade others of the benefits of becoming disciples. In other words, it was the place where evangelism happened. Thus, the Temple became the central focus of their social life and gathering in the Temple connected them with one another and with the greater community of the people of Jerusalem.

Second, while the Temple was the place of gathering, it is doubtful that it was their place of true worship, at least for any length of time. Worship in the Temple centered around offering sacrifices for atonement, petition, and thanksgiving. As the Christians began to interpret the meaning of Jesus' teachings, they realized that his death and resurrection made individual sacrifices irrelevant; Jesus was the ultimate sacrifice of atonement, the true Lamb of God that took away their Sin. In the weeks following Pentecost their focus would shift away from the Temple as a place of worship and toward a more intimate gathering that took place in the homes of the believers. There they shared the stories of Jesus' life and teachings, they recalled the words of the Hebrew scriptures, especially those of the prophets, in which they saw Jesus' ministry foretold, and they sang the songs of praise that gave voice to the emotions of their hearts. But most of all, they recalled and reclaimed the words and actions of the Last Supper, remembering the broken body and spilled blood that brought forth their salvation, sharing again in that holy moment as told to them by the original disciples. The home church had been given birth and a pattern of worship began to emerge, one that focused on the experience of the risen Christ.

We should note here, however, that the use of the singular word "church" is likely inappropriate. In the description of this early Church, Luke suggests that it quickly grew to number in the thousands; no home was big enough to host such numbers! A more accurate understanding would be that the homes of the apostles and first believers became a gathering place for small groups of new Christians and these home churches were scattered throughout the city. In fact, this scenario would become the paradigm for the new churches Paul would initiate throughout Syria, Asia, Macedonia, and Greece. In these small, intimate gatherings relationships would grow quickly and the people would become like family members to one another.

This, then, leads to a third point: the economic structure of the early church was a social-based model in which individual needs were cared for by the group as a whole. Each individual Christian contributed to the care of the needy and no-one went without the necessities of their lives. Perhaps this was an indispensable need at first, providing time for the Apostles to spend their energy spreading the good news rather than having to work to make their living. It may also have been the simple act of extending hospitality, a fact of life ingrained in their historical heritage. Yet as time passed, the Christians came to understand that sharing what they had with those in need fulfilled what Jesus lifted up as the second great commandment: " . . . *love your neighbor as you love yourself* "[1]. Thus, from the earliest days of the church, gathering for worship and fellowship was closely linked to taking care of one another, especially those in need.

Doing Church

In today's world, perhaps it is the small, rural church that most closely resembles that of the early apostles. That is not to say that larger or urban churches are not valid, real, or effective; they are. Rather, this observation is to affirm some of the inherent values of the churches found scattered

1. Matthew 22:39

throughout the countryside, values that are often ignored or forgotten. Like the church that emerged in the days following the Pentecost experience, the heart of these churches is expressed in three things: worship, intimate relationships, and care for one another.

Small church sanctuaries, like the Temple, are the places where God's people gather to worship. Many of those sanctuaries were ill-conceived, by modern standards, and virtually all are inflexible. The people sit in pews, rigidly fixed to the floor in rows that face the preacher. The pulpit occupies the focal point of the sanctuary, emphasizing the primacy of the proclaimed Word. The sacredness of the space is lifted up by crosses, pictures, and stained-glass windows, many of which have plaques attached to them that say, "*In Memory of* _____." The acoustics are poor and, unless improvements have been made in recent years, the space is cold in the winter and hot in the summer. Many have a bell, harkening back to a time when it was used to call the people together from the surrounding countryside. And yes, white seems to be the preferred exterior color. Yet these sanctuaries are incredibly special, and heaven help the young preacher who suggests that changes need to be made in order to make worship more relevant!

These sanctuaries are sacred spaces, made so by the fact that it is here that faithful disciples re-connect with God on a weekly basis and new believers come to experience the power of the Holy Spirit. Their sacredness is not in the design or theological appropriateness of the space, but in the warm memories and institutional values they represent. The worship that takes place in these spaces may be, by some standards, old fashioned and outdated, but for the saints of these churches it recalls the significant moments of their lives and the people who made those moments special. Like the disciples re-presenting the last supper to recall the sacrifice of Christ, weekly worship in the small church is an opportunity to remember who they are and why they have come together. Certainly, this memory comes from the routine and rehearsed style of worship, often from the music of decades passed, but it comes primarily from the fact that it happens in a place that most consider to be their "home."

Yet the sanctuaries are not the only place where the small church congregation gathers. This is truly the place of worship, but evangelism happens in other places. The focus of this book is on the small church located in a rural or town and country setting, and these settings have their own uniqueness. On any given day of the week one can venture to a local restaurant or coffee shop to find a cadre of farmers or local business owners or retired persons gathered around a table, swapping stories and sharing life. Friday nights in the fall, virtually the whole town turns out for the high school football game. The calendar year is punctuated by community gatherings on special holidays like Christmas and Memorial Day or the Fourth of July. Pastors often find that their best opportunity for pastoral care comes from a visit to the local grocery store. Like the disciples in the Temple, being with the community in these settings is an opportunity to connect with those within the church as well as those outside the church, to discover the needs and concerns of the community and to become a visible witness of faith to others, and the pastor often finds people who have never been to "church" identifying with the congregation. The point here is that the opportunity to be together extends beyond a short time on Sunday morning and it is in these places that the people of God intersect with the people of the world, not to just invite them to church, but to hear their needs, to share their joys, to build relationships that bear fruit. This is the heart of productive evangelism. Most certainly this can and does happen in larger churches and urban communities, but the opportunity is built into the fabric of the small church and its community.

Out of this interaction comes a sense of intimacy that fosters deep relationships and out of these relationships comes a sense of caring and connection. A visitor once expressed to the pastor of a small church: *"I love coming here; I feel Jesus."* Having come from a larger church where people gathered in small groups and visited among themselves, she was overwhelmed by the fact that *everyone* in this small church greeted her, hugged her, and offered her an opportunity for a relationship through their warmth and caring. In a larger congregation, one can come in and remain somewhat anonymous: not so in a small church. Being with the same people on a regular basis builds relationships and out of these relationships care for one another grows. If someone in the congregation is absent, the others notice. If someone in the congregation is ill, the concern is shared. If someone needs help, efforts are made to provide the necessary aid. Many of these churches take pride in talking about their church "family," which is a way of expressing the intimacy of the relationships that have been formed. The pastor of one of these small churches describes his congregation in these words: *"Here, everybody has a story, and everybody else knows that story . . . but loves them anyway!"* Like a family, the intimate relationships formed within these small congregations provide love, affection, support, concern, and hope, with members accepting one another for who they are and caring for them as they would care for their own families.

Yet the majority of small churches do not understand the advantage of their size and the opportunities within their communities. They have bought into the myth that bigger is better and feel that their little world is insignificant in the grand scheme of things. Often their strength goes unnoticed by those outside their communities and their leadership is not recognized by their judicatory or the larger church. Their constituency never grows in large numbers and even the aggregate membership of small churches within an entire county is less than that of a larger church in an urban setting. Their ability to fund and staff ministries that impact large crowds is usually lacking and what ministries are present for the community are typically small, though effective. Together these characteristics create a self-image that fails to honor the real core values of the church and cannot appreciate the strength of leadership that is present.

Seeing Church

A young man, recently graduated from seminary, was excited about his first pastorate, a rural congregation of about 80 members that was over 100 years old. Armed with the latest research in church growth and urban development, he was prepared to provide the catalyst for this church to grow by leaps and bounds. In seminary, he was lauded for his preaching, honored by his professors for his far-reaching exegesis and his dynamic style of delivery, and he was anxious to bring these skills to the people of his church, convinced that his people were about to receive preaching like they had never heard before and that his message would bring the growth that he knew was about to come.

At his first meeting of the church council, he shared his hopes for the church, hopes that became contagious within the leadership. They, too, became excited about the potential for the church, so they were anxious to support him and give him what he needed to fulfill their dreams. One of those things was a sign he requested at the front door: *"Enter in silence, prepared to meet God."* Referring to the call of Isaiah and the theophany he experienced in the Temple, he explained to the council that he wanted everyone to encounter God as the *"Mysterium Tremendum."* The leadership graciously received his request but had no idea what he was talking about.

61

The sign was made and placed over the front door leading into the sanctuary. His sermon that week was based on the sixth chapter of Isaiah, which he had referenced in the meeting, and he made a valiant effort to explain what Rudolph Otto had meant in his words describing the "*Mysterium Tremendum,*" just as he had been taught in his seminary classes. In his sermon, he described what he believed to be ideal worship: the people come into the sanctuary, the "Holy of Holies," with awe and reverence, knowing that God is present and that a true experience of God awaits them. But, while all this sounded wonderful from the pulpit, the practical application of his ideas was not as well received.

Like virtually all small congregations, Sunday morning had the feel of a family reunion in his church. People greeted one another boldly, caught up on what was going on in their families, and playfully, but lovingly, poked fun at one another. Rather than the quiet, serene, and meditative space he envisioned the sanctuary was more like a beehive as the members of the congregation moved about in a flurry of conversation. The young pastor was disappointed that his flock had neither heard nor received his message of the sacredness of worship and verbal reminders seemed to have no effect. He, therefore, decided on a new tactic to get his point across. Ten minutes before the worship service began, he came into the sanctuary, knelt at the altar, and prayed until it was time to begin, thinking that, surely, seeing him in prayer would bring out the respect of his congregation and silence would result. It worked. Within a few weeks the pre-worship time fell silent. As this began to happen, he praised the congregation and invited others to join him in prayer, and several did, coming forward to the altar as they entered the sanctuary, kneeling or standing to offer a silent prayer for the pastor and the worship service. The young, new pastor was pleased at the results his model produced. However, one Sunday morning his praying became distracted by the sound of several men talking in the back of the sanctuary. Although he could not hear their exact words, he recognized their voices and became determined to confront them. Rising from his place at the altar, he moved in a determined fashion to where the men were gathered, his anger evident to all in the sanctuary.

His first words communicated his feelings: they were extremely rude in violating the quietness of the sanctuary and disturbing this time of prayer and worship. "*Son, do you have any idea what we were talking about?*" was the reply from one of the older men, a key leader in the church.

Mrs. Atkins lives down the road from me. She's a single mother with three kids to take care of. Last night her milk cow busted through the fence and tore an udder. Now, she depends on that cow to provide milk for her kids and the butter she makes gives her a little help paying for groceries. She needs our help, and we were trying to figure out what we could do. After church I'm going to go by and pick up her cow and take it to the vet. Harry's agreed to fix the fence and make sure the pasture is secure and Tom's agreed to let her borrow one of his cows until hers' is able to be milked again. Now, that may not seem very important to you, but without our help she'd be in a world of hurt. We felt like arranging to help her was more important than praying at the moment; we've done that and we're ready to worship, if you are.

In this encounter, the young pastor was given the opportunity to understand his church and his congregation in a new way; the lesson he learned would shape his understanding of the relationship between worship and service for the rest of his ministry. It also gave him a respect for his leaders, who were much more anxious to express love than talk about it.

A New Perspective

While the young pastor in the above story was well intentioned and quite brilliant, he overlooked the very things that made his small, rural church strong and that had enabled the congregation to survive and thrive for over a hundred years: community. It is a mistake made by many pastors and even some of the churches themselves. While the myth "bigger is better" may apply in some things and, occasionally, in churches, to buy into this myth is to deny the legacy of the majority of churches in service today, as well as the majority of churches within the Christian tradition. There is a uniqueness in small churches that gives them an inherent strength: ignoring or battling against that strength leads to tension and brokenness; building on that strength leads to a productive small church.

A quick perusal of church growth literature today reveals that the vast majority of what is written focuses on large churches in urban areas, out of which grow what are often called "mega-churches." Yet, while garnering the bulk of the attention, these churches actually constitute less than one half of one percent of congregations in North America, with an average attendance of less than one tenth of one percent on any given Sunday. On the other hand, small churches, defined as those that average less than 100 in worship, constitute 59% of the churches and the median attendance for all churches is 75 persons.[2] Not only do small churches make up the majority of congregations, but they also most resemble the church in the days of its beginning, focusing on worship, intimate relationships, and care for one another. Instead of focusing our attention on the problems of being small, we need to lift up the advantages and learn how to use those advantages to become productive. One author has done that.

In his book The Strategically Small Church, Brandon O'Brien has rather boldly lifted up the advantages of being small and how to capitalize on those advantages.[3] He identifies four strengths that are unique to the small church: intimacy; nimbleness; authenticity; and effectiveness. Each of these is worthy of further reflection.

Intimacy thrives in the midst of smallness. True intimacy fosters productive ministry. Out of close relationships, opportunities for ministries of caring abound. In families there is no need to engage in a process of needs assessment because the needs and desires of the others in the relationship are evident; it is the same in the small church. The closeness of the congregation creates relationships in which the needs and desires of the others are evident, and these needs are real, not imagined or deduced. Many small churches include a time in their worship for the sharing of joys and concerns: just as a family would around the dinner table, the congregation uses this opportunity to share in the lives of those whom they love. This same closeness extends beyond the world of the sanctuary into the local community. Small churches extend their love into the area surrounding the church, knowing that the recipients of their love are not strangers, but neighbors, with whom they work, whose children share their schools, who shop in the same stores. Christian caring leads the church to reach out into the community because the people there are like—and sometimes actually are—an extended family. The suffering of others brings suffering to the whole church and the joy of others is shared by all. This is true intimacy, an almost inescapable product of being small, which even larger churches are beginning to seek through intentional small group ministries.

There is, however, a downside to smallness and intimacy that can deter productivity in ministry. Close relationships and the expression of caring can easily morph into gossip and the very information that can lead

2. © 2000 - 2018 Hartford Seminary, Hartford Institute for Religion Research. www.hartfordinstitute.org.

3. O'Brien *The Strategically Small Church, 2010.*

to helping others may become an instrument of their suffering. While expressing concern openly invites others to share in those concerns, it is an ever-present possibility that the inappropriate expression of one another's struggles can cause pain. Therefore, this strength of the small church must be appropriately managed by its leadership. Responsible management can be achieved through a constant awareness of the sacred trust that has been given through the intimacy of the relationships and the rights and feelings of those named in the concerns. Before information is shared openly or even through private conversation, it should be vetted. Pastors should, as a habit, ask individuals for permission to share their concerns; the amount of information that is shared should be limited; gossip should be eliminated. Also, extreme care should be exercised in the disclosure of names and personal information through print and electronic media. Many churches include a tab on their webpage for the expression of joys and concerns, or a use a Facebook page: access to this information should be restricted from the general public and any party that might misuse the information.

Furthermore, in addition to the sharing of information, churches would do well to invite appropriate responses to the needs and joys expressed: visits, phone calls, cards, texts, etc. Intimacy only happens in the midst of personal contact. It is in these responses that intimacy is built and maintained as people connect with one another in the most vulnerable moments of their lives. Often, a simple note sent in a time of need is remembered years after the contact was made. Broken relationships are healed when persons reach out to one another and overcome barriers of separation. Finally, when persons are respected as one would the member of one's own family, it becomes natural to see past the stereotypes and judgments of others and accept people for who they are.

Small churches are nimble. Consider the difference between an ocean liner and a small pleasure craft: the turning radius of a large ship may be a half-mile and requires both advanced planning and time for execution; a small boat can reverse course in a matter of moments and within a few yards distance. Of necessity, larger churches rely on bureaucracy for their administration and decisions must go through layers of consideration before they are implemented to ensure proper management of the church's resources. In a typical scenario, new ministries begin with an idea from an individual or small group in the church, which is referred to the appropriate committee to be considered and shaped, then to those responsible for financial management for funding, then to the church council or appropriate legislative body for approval, then back to a task force for implementation. All this takes time and energy and, while ensuring successful ministries, requires that the church plan well ahead of the time of need. With a smaller church, the time between idea and implementation can be measured in days, sometimes even hours, rather than weeks or months.

An example of nimbleness can be seen in a recent event at a small church. The first Sunday of each month is designated as the time for celebrating the sacrament of communion and the congregation is invited to make a special donation, referred to as a "communion rail offering," that is used to support local missions. The missions team schedules which ministries are to receive this offering and publicizes this information a month in advance so the congregation can plan accordingly. On one such Sunday, during the time of sharing joys and concerns, it was made known that the relative of a church member had been in a car accident and was hospitalized and that he would be off work for quite some time. On hearing this, one of the church members asked, *"Is there something the church can do for him?"* The missions chair suggested that they could use that day's communion rail offering for some financial assistance, the rest of the team agreed, and it was done. The entire process took less than two minutes and the church responded to the need in an effective manner. This type of nimble decision making is much easier in the small church, wherein the stakeholders are together on a regular basis outside of formal meetings, and it can provide benefits beyond the obvious: in addition to the effective response, the members of the congregation became intimately connected to the one in need and his family.

In addition to enabling the church to respond to perceived needs, a sense of nimbleness also enables the members of the congregation to anticipate needs even before they are expressed. Combining this anticipation with a true sense of intimacy often leads members of the church into acts of kindness, charity, and service before being asked or informed of the need. Larger churches need committees and task forces to accomplish even the most routine functions of the church and much time is spent administering the programs, assigning responsibilities, and reminding people of their commitments; often in small churches tasks just get done. It is not uncommon in small churches, especially those in rural settings, to have individuals who take upon themselves care of the lawn or the printing of bulletins or setting up tables for lunches as a personal ministry. These people are not assigned their tasks and sometimes others in the church do not even know that they are the ones doing the work; they simply and humbly anticipate the need and take care of it, without fanfare or recognition.

While much more prevalent in the small church, however, nimbleness is not an inevitable trait; it must be nurtured, and it can only be effective in the presence of trusting relationships. Without a trust in one another, it is difficult to make healthy decisions, especially those that affect the direction of the congregation. True intimacy in a congregation creates an environment of trust that allows the people to make decisions and respond to needs without layers of bureaucracy. Yet some churches cling to a rigid structure of leadership that forces layered decision making and often delays action and implementation, becoming an adversary of nimbleness and even fostering attitudes of defensiveness and mistrust. This does not, however, suggest that formal decision-making processes are or should be ignored or abandoned, only that, when faced with opportunities, the small church is able to respond more rapidly because of the very nature of being small: people can communicate with one another more rapidly and share a common concern for the ministries of the church that can be expressed openly. Therefore, churches that seek to become more productive in their ministry should take the time and energy to analyze their decision-making process and seek to make it as streamlined as possible, building on the intimate trust of one another and focusing on the need to make disciples rather than the need to maintain structures.

Authenticity is a hallmark of the small church. Sometimes expressed as integrity, it is the quality of being real. It is the integration of faith and practice, of personality and action. Some might also use the term transparency, the ability to see through the outside in order to know what's on the inside. In many small churches there is an unwritten, but often spoken, motto: *"What you see is what you get."* Whether the inner spirit of a church is good or bad, positive or negative, healthy or unhealthy, its qualities are easy to perceive, mainly because there is no place to hide. While the intricacies of authenticity are complex and far-reaching, the values of it are unmistakable. In a current culture where "fake news" is a commonly spoken phrase and obvious mistruths are put forward in order to shape the images of people and institutions, there is a deep-seated yearning for truth, honesty, and integrity. Here, the small church has an asset that works to its advantage.

Brandon O'Brien tells a tale of one of his pastorates, which other pastors can echo in their own experience. At a small church in the middle of nowhere, the music program was sorely lacking in quality and depth. Their repertoire consisted of a handful of songs from a by-gone era, whose words were not even in the vocabulary of most of the parishioners. His preaching was mediocre at best, lacking the stage presence of a seasoned professional. Worship fell way short of what anyone would call spectacular, yet people came because "... *we were ourselves – unashamedly, unapologetically, unalterably ourselves."* In his analysis, Rev. O'Brien observes that the glitz and glam of highly polished worship has given way to a hunger for realness, in which people are free to share their hurts and hopes, successes and failures, without feeling like they have to be something that they are not and that the small church is in a strategic position to offer this quality. [4]

However, the small church should not view this as an excuse for mediocrity; rather, it should strive to lift out the best qualities of its inherent personality and not try to simply live off its image. The true authenticity of the small church stems from the fact that, absent of ample resources to fund professionals, the church must rely on volunteers, giving the opportunity for the people in the pews to invest themselves personally in the ministry of the church. In this way, the people connect with that ministry and find themselves living out the truth that they hear in the gospel. Thus, they need not look at others and ask, *"Are they real?"* but look at themselves and proclaim *"I am who I am ... I am who God made me to be."* In other words, the authenticity and integrity of the church become manifest in the people themselves as they discover a very real God in the midst of their sometimes embarrassingly real lives as faith and action are wedded; not in a performance of professionals, but in the personal experience of ministry. In this, the small church becomes the living example of what the author of James lifts up as the example of faith: "... *but be doers of the word and not hearers only, thereby deceiving yourselves."*[5]

Intimacy, nimbleness and authenticity, therefore, combine to help make the small church effective. The qualities of the church that are expressed in these three descriptors lead the congregation to be effective in their ministry, to produce fruit. Too often small churches, in their desire to become big, attempt to become something that they are not, duplicating programs and strategies that are beyond their means and that belie the very nature of who they are. Yet churches that recognize their strengths and capitalize on the advantage of their size are able to use these qualities to make a difference in the lives of others and, thereby, to make disciples. The key to a

4. O'Brien, pp. 57-59

5. James 1:22

productive church rests in its ability to be honest in its self-assessment, to accept its identity and to raise up leaders who can and will motivate others to live out their faith in an authentic way.

Yet effectiveness cannot be measured against arbitrary standards imposed from external sources, which is a trait that is too often present among small churches. Productive ministries in one context may take on a shape and personality that is totally different and unique from those in other settings. The small church must rid itself of comparison evaluation, holding itself accountable by measures of success in other contexts. Instead, it must be guided by its own unique vision and allow that vision to be the standard against which its effectiveness is measured. In other words, the church must both find and own its unique identity, building on its strengths instead of decrying or apologizing for its weaknesses. The ultimate question of productive ministry is, once again, *"Does it make disciples?"* and any church that can answer "yes" to this question is a productive church.

Setting Out for Deeper Waters

Through the proper recognition and leverage of its strengths, the small church places itself in a strategic position for becoming productive. Rather than a barrier to effective ministry, smallness may actually become an advantage, its inherent qualities of intimacy, nimbleness and authenticity giving rise to productive ministry. How these qualities are used is a function of leadership and productive leadership builds on these and other qualities in order to make disciples, but doing so often requires a shift in traditional understandings of leadership in the church.

Growing Leadership

Productive leadership in the small church is possible only when the church is willing to honestly evaluate itself and its ministries. This section invites the leaders of the church to make that honest assessment and to claim the strengths that can enable the church to move forward in ministry. The following exercises challenge church leaders to accomplish this task.

a. How small is our church? Using the continuum below, note where your church falls.

HOW BIG ARE WE?				
Tiny	Small	Average	Large	Mega

➤

Mega	-	Worship attendance: over 2,000	0.5% of churches in North America
Large	-	Worship attendance: 500–2,000	5%
Average	-	Worship Attendance: 100–500	30%
Small/Tiny	-	Worship attendance: less than 100	65%

b. Make an honest assessment of your size; do you consider the church's size to be an advantage or a barrier?

c. What are the inherent strengths of your congregation? How do they enable you to make disciples?

d. What are the inherent weaknesses of your congregation? How do they hinder you from making disciples?

e. Outline the typical process for decision making in your church, especially with regard to the development of new ministries, noting the stakeholders involved in the process and a typical timeline for implementation. Along with this, create a flow chart of the steps taken in the decision-making process, including committees and groups in the church that are consulted. Use this outline to address the following issues.

- How and where are decisions made in your church? How are those decisions communicated to the membership?

- Does the structure of your leadership enhance or deter quality decisions?

- When was the last time your church considered changes in the leadership structure?

- What could be done to streamline your decision-making process?

f. Honestly evaluate your church with regard to the four qualities lifted up by Brandon O'Brien. On a scale of 1 to 10, where would you place your church regarding:

- Intimacy

- Nimbleness

- Authenticity
- Effectiveness

g. What could you do to increase the presence of each of these qualities?

7

Leadership in the Productive Church

Saul became increasingly more powerful and confounded the Jews who lived in Damascus by proving that Jesus was the Messiah.

After some time had passed, the Jews plotted to kill him, but their plot became known to Saul. They were watching the gates day and night so that they might kill him; but his disciples took him by night and let him down through an opening in the wall, lowering him in a basket.

When he had come to Jerusalem, he attempted to join the disciples; and they were all afraid of him, for they did not believe that he was a disciple. But Barnabas took him, brought him to the apostles, and described for them how on the road he had seen the Lord, who had spoken to him, and how in Damascus he had spoken boldly in the name of Jesus. So he went in and out among them in Jerusalem, speaking boldly in the name of the Lord. He spoke and argued with the Hellenists; but they were attempting to kill him. When the believers learned of it, they brought him down to Caesarea and sent him off to Tarsus.

—ACTS 9:22–30

IN THE EARLY DAYS of the church, Paul was a clear enemy of the Christians. As the story unfolds in the Book of Acts, it is this ardent pharisee from Tarsus that takes upon himself the mission of destroying the emerging band of believers, standing off to the side during the stoning of Stephen, then hunting down Christians in the extended reaches of the Palestinian world. Is it any wonder that the Apostles would not receive him, that they were afraid of him? With just cause, they sought to exclude Paul from their company, knowing that he had the potential to personally arrest and even execute them and bring destruction to the still-emerging Church. The leadership of the Apostles put them in the role of gatekeeper, preserving the present safety of the believers and the future history of the Christian movement. While they went about their daily lives telling the stories of Jesus and bringing others to belief, while they saw to it that those among their numbers that had needs were cared for, they also saw themselves as the ones in control, using the authority of their commission to ensure the future of the Church. Yet the apostles were not the only leaders in the story.

Barnabas was a leader. Having heard the story of Paul's conversion, having heard the preaching of Paul as he convinced the Jews in Damascus that Jesus was, indeed, the Messiah, having witnessed Paul's determination to carry out his new mission, Barnabas understood that God was at work in and through this former persecutor of the Christians. Risking his own reputation and relationship with the apostles, Barnabas stepped up in Paul's defense and convinced Peter and the others that Paul could be trusted. His argument was founded on one reality: God was working through Paul. He alone, it seems, was able to see beyond the need for caution and separation in order to realize that, through Paul, God could do great things. The Christian Church was shaped by the preaching of Paul, his extensive missionary travels, his boldness in the face of opposition and the astute theological reflection of his letters, but without Barnabas, Paul would have remained as an outcast. Who knows what the Church would have become if Barnabas had not stepped up as a leader?

In this story we can see contrasting focuses of leadership, one of which builds barriers of defense in fear, while the other steps forward in boldness. One set of leaders serves as the gatekeeper, protecting the status quo, while the other opens the door to new possibilities, based on the evidence of God's work. This assessment of the leadership of Peter and the apostles is not intended to criticize or condemn them for their fears, which were very real, but to raise an awareness of what happens when those fears blind us from seeing the work God is doing, especially through others who are different and who we might even consider to be the enemy. Barnabas did not fear Paul because he had seen God at work in Paul's life, which gave him a vision of possibility. Perhaps this vision can be expressed as a vision of the future kingdom of God that was possible through Paul, a sense of true hopefulness in what God could do. This is productive leadership.

Doing Church

What makes a person a leader in the church? While the answer to this question can easily fill a book on its own, put very simply, leaders lead. That is, church leaders are the ones who step up to take responsibility for the life, health, and direction of their congregation. While most of these leaders are out front and visible, their leadership easily and readily recognized by others, many lead in discreet ways, unassumingly directing the path of the church and its ministry behind the scenes. People like Desmond Tutu and Billy Graham were clear leaders, who were out front and visible in their work, calling others to follow them in the quest of their mission, but so were people like Mother Theresa, who humbly served and, by her example, led others to commitment. Some lead through the exercise of authority, some by empowering others, some by their own service and witness and some by the example they set for others. In other words, leadership comes in many different forms and there is not a single style of leadership that sets people apart as effective leaders. There is, however, one test of leadership that is foolproof: *do others follow?* Leaders who have no followers are not leaders. Therefore, if you would like to know if you are a leader, look over your shoulder . . . if no one is following you, you are not a leader!

While we like to image leaders as the head of companies or corporations, as dynamic women and men who persuade others to take action, sometimes as heroes that step up in a time of need, there is no one image of a leader that can describe what leadership is. In fact, the styles of leadership are as varied as the leaders themselves and the effectiveness of each of the styles depends on the ability of the person to use their style of leadership at the right time and in the right way. An effective leader in one setting may fail to lead in another; a follower in one may become a leader in another. In Bearing Fruit, the authors name three descriptors of effective leadership that have emerged out of the work of the Lewis Center at Wesley Theological Seminary: Character, Competence and Contribution.[1] These descriptors create a handy framework for discussing leadership, giving us a lens through which we can view the qualities of effective leaders and they will shape the organization of the next three chapters. We begin, however, by looking at leadership in the small church and how it is typically viewed.

It would be unfair to say that small churches raise up more or better leaders. However, it holds true that leadership in the small church takes on

---

1 Weems and Beringer, *Bearing Fruit*, p.xiii.

a different character. Just as the small church tends to exhibit qualities that work to its advantage—nimbleness, intimacy, authenticity, and effectiveness—leaders in these churches seem to bring forth the same qualities that work to their advantage. Indeed, the nature of the church itself is often a mirror of the nature of its leaders. Of necessity, small churches must rely on the leadership within the church for their survival, given the fact that many of them, especially in denominations that assign their pastors, have a rapid rate of turnover in pastoral leadership. It is not uncommon for the pastor of the church, especially those serving in a part time capacity, to live outside the parish. Unless they have grown up within the community, most pastors of these churches are outsiders and must rely on the lay leadership to establish connections within their particular setting. In churches that are on a circuit, the pastor is not always available when the needs arise and often makes a long drive between services at the various stations, so the bulk of the worship service is carried out by the laity, leaving the preaching and sacraments to the assigned pastor. Also, in the absence of a pastor—such as a period between calls or assignments—the church continues in worship and ministry through its lay leadership, often quite effectively. And, while it would be an injustice to pastoral leaders to say that the church could function better without them, in many cases it falls upon the lay leaders to continue the life of the church in the face of absent, distracted or faltering leadership from their pastor. It is safe to say that many small churches are alive and thriving today because of the quality and effectiveness of their lay leadership: the fact that many of them have survived for over a century is a testimony to that leadership.

The presence of good leadership, however, does not automatically imply that the leadership is productive. Peter and James were good leaders, but when Paul was brought before them, it was Barnabas who moved toward productivity. The leadership of the Apostles was focused on preserving and protecting the new Church, expanding into the community around them through their evangelism, while Barnabas saw a larger picture of possibilities in what God was already doing. Peter and James were focused on what was best for the community; Barnabas focused on what was best for the Kingdom. Often, local church leaders become focused on themselves, their needs and their immediate context, especially when confronted by crises and extenuating circumstances. In an effort to preserve and protect the church they love they move toward decisions that guard against change. Their leadership is good and, in so far as it accomplishes the goal of self-preservation, it is effective, yet it falls short of being productive because it fails to truly make disciples. Furthermore, leadership is a dynamic enterprise, always evolving and shifting as both the individual and the circumstances change.

Many people have written about the life cycle of churches and the changing needs of local church ministry. A typical model reflects a period of rapid growth, followed by time of leveling off, then gradual decline. This life cycle may also be seen in terms of infancy, middle age, and old age. The graph of this life cycle—which is actually a pattern rather than a cycle—is a bell curve that begins in the birth and eventually ends in the death of the church. As the congregation is established, there is a wave of excitement that compels the membership to reach out and include others. The efforts and intention of the church are focused upon evangelism and gatherings are punctuated by a healthy, welcoming attitude toward others. Over a period of time, however, relationships are established, an intimacy develops within the community and the gathering of the church becomes like a family reunion as the need to include others lessens. The growth and outward ministry of the church begins to diminish while the church reaches a plateau. During this period of time the church becomes stable and well established. What follows is inevitable decline as the church begins to pay the price for its lack of productivity, for as the congregation loses members and leaders to natural attrition, they begin to experience hardship and a poverty in available workers in the church. Without an impetus to change their perspective, the congregation and its leaders shift into a survival mode, focusing themselves inward toward the preservation of the institution, the family, and the values they hold in common.

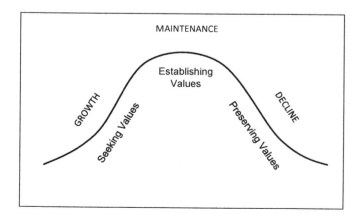

This image applies to church leadership as well. In the growing phase of the church, leadership is being explored and developed as new people enter into the life of the congregation. There is an openness to new ideas and perspectives and new opportunities for ministry are welcomed and encouraged. Just as the church as a whole seeks to find its value and place in the community, leaders seek to discover their identity within the congregation and how they can best offer their gifts to the ministry of the church. Successes in ministry fuel the desire to do more, so the leadership constantly seeks out ways in which the church can develop new ministries and capitalize on new opportunities for growth. The excitement of growing breeds commitment and church leadership becomes a high priority in the life of the congregation.

As the life of the church reaches a plateau, the leadership begins to shift. Relationships have already been established, so the focus moves toward strengthening existing bonds between individuals rather than establishing new friends. The excitement of developing new ministries gives way to the routine work of managing existing programs. Having found their values, the leadership begins to hold those values up as a banner under which the congregation lives. The roster of church leaders becomes full and there is little need to seek out and develop new leaders. The work of the church loses its challenge, and the thrill of victory moves commitment to a lower priority. In the comfort of an established and healthy church, complacency begins to set in. The church is doing well, so the need for individual leadership loses its necessity.

Once complacency rears its ugly head, decline inevitably follows. Without an influx of new leadership, existing leaders become tired and sometimes bored. Many of these leaders have aged in place and no longer have the energy to continue giving themselves to the church in the way to which they, and the church, are accustomed. Natural attrition takes its toll on the number of leaders and, in the absence of efforts to develop new leadership, the work of ministry falls to fewer and fewer individuals, many of whom are already stretched to their limit. Feelings of ingratitude begin to emerge as the leaders undertake thankless tasks and many that were once the bulwarks of the church either abdicate their leadership roles or quit the church altogether. As the incomes of older members begin to wain financial resources decline. Coupled with the attrition of the congregation and the lack of commitment among the leaders, the problems of decline are compounded even further, adding to the stress.

Seeing the end of the church on the horizon, the remaining leadership begins to live in fear of losing the life they once had and begins to commit themselves to preserving the church and its values. A spirit of grief begins to overtake the congregation as they share in the loss of friends, of the values they hold dearly, and of relationships in which they find their meaning. Gatherings of the congregation, once punctuated by a joyous and open spirit, are now characterized by defensiveness as hope for the future wanes. Once on the distant horizon, the death of the church becomes imminent and the mourning begins. The once productive church has met its demise. Without something to break the momentum of this pattern and change the perspective of the church, it is the fate that awaits every small church.

Seeing Church

The small church was thriving, riding a wave of growth it had not seen in over three decades. To meet the needs of the growing congregation, a new fellowship hall, including a large kitchen and a few classrooms, had been added and was being used almost constantly, both by the church and by the community. But building this addition had not been an easy accomplishment for the congregation, pitting the newcomers—mostly baby-boomers—against the old guard, most of whom grew up in the depression and war years. There was no question about the need for the new space; the issue was paying for it. The newcomers were quite willing to finance the entire amount, over a half-million dollars, while the veteran leaders ran from any indebtedness at all. A compromise was reached: ground was broken for the new building only after half of the funds were already raised and the cash was in the bank; the remaining portion was financed. While adding the mortgage payment stretched the finances of the church, it was successfully managed through constant diligence and some additional fund-raising. Several large gifts to the church enabled them to retire the debt after only five years and the congregation, especially the old guard, breathed a sigh of relief.

A very short time later, a new opportunity arose: a building adjacent to the church property became available when the business decided to relocate to a new facility. Unlike the previous project, the church did not need this space since it was quite comfortable in its recent expansion. There was a lot of informal conversation among the members of the church, but no formal action from the church council was taken toward acquiring this property. That, however, did not stop the gossip and the rumor was circulated that the church was going to purchase the property, which began to raise the ire of the older membership of the church: they had just suffered through a period of indebtedness and feared that adding a new debt would bring the demise of the church, all for an unnecessary purchase. Their fear was based on the fact that they, the older membership of the church, were aging and could not afford the increased financial responsibility and they did not trust the young families to carry the load. In the midst of the gossip and rumors, Ken came to see the pastor.

Ken was a leader in the church but did not accept his own leadership. He shunned any formal positions, detested meetings and, for the most part, did not participate in any of the church politics. However, he was quick to lend a hand whenever there was a physical need at the church, building playgrounds, painting classrooms, or demolishing old storage buildings. In the previous building program, he had been a strong voice against indebtedness, so, disturbed by the fact that the church might incur a debt for a building that they did not need, he was prepared to raise his voice again. Yet he did not come to the pastor with an agenda; his visit to the pastor was more of a fact-finding mission than anything else. After hearing for himself that there were currently no plans to purchase the property, he was satisfied and began to share the facts with his contemporaries, putting an end to the rumors and easing the tension that he had perceived, a move welcomed by the pastor. But the conversation did not end with that visit.

A few days later, Ken revisited the topic, asking why the church council had decided to forego purchase of the property and if there was any discussion about how the property might be used. Once again, the pastor shared the discussions about finances and that the council felt like the church could not afford it at this time. The next week, Ken showed up in the pastor's office once again and wanted to continue the discussion. The leading question caught the pastor by surprise: *"What's the next step for the church? What new ministries would you like to see the church begin?"* Since the relationship between the two had always been open and honest, the pastor laid out what he felt were the next steps for the church's ministry: attention to youth ministries and a program of community outreach designed to teach basic skills in finances, childcare, and employment seeking, all of which were a part of the church's long range plans. *"If we bought the building, could it be used for these ministries?"* Ken asked. After a short conversation, the two agreed that half the space could be used to create a sizable youth center with little effort, and the other half remodeled to create classrooms for community education, a resource center that could help people find and apply for employment, a workshop to facilitate church repairs, and a small area where he and some of the older men could gather for coffee during the week. It was at that time that he revealed that he had been talking to the owner of the building, who was willing to sell it to the church below the market value, provided they could make a decision before he moved his business out, expected to be within the month. He then said, *"Preacher, I know that you and the council don't think we can afford to buy this building, but we can't afford not to buy it if we want this church to continue to grow."*

Armed with the information about how the building could be used, Ken started talking behind the scenes, seeking to convince his generation of church members that they needed to purchase this property to ensure the church's future. Rumors that once caused concern among the older members gave way to a new excitement about the possibilities and, at the next meeting of the church council, the decision was made to make the purchase. Before the papers were signed, Ken and his circle of leaders had raised the funds to make a sizable down payment on the building, secured pledges to cover the monthly indebtedness, and identified resources to help with remodeling.

A New Perspective

In this story can be seen how a church can move from comfort and complacency to a sense of excitement about emerging possibilities, and how excitement about those possibilities can elevate the commitment of persons to accomplish goals once thought unreachable. Unknowingly, Ken's willingness to discover the truth created an openness that unlocked the door to a new vision and he and the older members of the church began to look past themselves and their needs and values in order to see the possibilities of the greater Kingdom of God. He would not consider himself a leader, yet he led the congregation into a new and exciting range of ministry that would enable it to be productive in years to come. He, almost single-handedly, had created a situation that shifted the life cycle of the church, ensuring that the decline that inevitably seems to follow stability and complacency gave way to a new excitement in reaching out to others, an acceptance of a new set of values in the life of the church, and a new opportunity for developing leadership, all of which resulted in productive ministry.

Therefore, in considering true leadership, there are several myths that need to be overcome, the first of which is that *leadership resides in an office*. While it is true that offices in the church, filled by elected or assigned laypersons, provide the opportunity to lead, they do not guarantee that the person holding the office is a leader. Too often, persons are given a position of leadership in the hopes that they will become a leader, but this practice is not healthy for the church. Leadership is the product of the character, skills, and competence of the person, combined to provide direction, decisions, and hope to others; being in a particular office may provide the opportunity to exercise these traits and apply them to the life of the church, but the traits themselves must come from within the person. Furthermore, true leaders don't need the authority of an office, but a vision of the future and the willingness to strive toward that vision.

Leaders are born, not made. While it is true that some persons have inherent qualities that contribute to good leadership, it is also true that persons can, and must, be trained in order to bring out the best of these qualities. With proper training and support, people can learn how to be leaders. The best practices of small churches include regular times of leadership development that provide opportunities for people to exercise their abilities and learn how to best use their skills in the ministry of the church.

Leadership can be given. No: offices and responsibility can be given, but leadership must be earned. Leadership is not about titles and honors; it is about people. Without trust, people do not follow and without followers, there are no leaders. Therefore, leadership must be earned through eliciting confidence from others and this can only happen by guiding the church toward the fulfillment of its mission, which actually means moving the people to follow the direction set, giving them confidence in the vision and motivating them to share in the common life of the shared ministry. Effective leaders use their office and responsibility to accomplish all this, but the ability to lead comes from the trust they exude before others.

Leadership comes from having authority. Once again, this myth falls short of reality. Authority can be given, but leadership must be earned. Simply being in charge does not make a person a leader any more than owning a car makes a person a good driver. Authority positions a person for the use of leadership, providing an opportunity for the exercise of skills and expression of values that move toward the accomplishment of a vision, but how those skills are used determines the productivity of leaders. Yet how often are we guilty of bestowing authority on persons, thinking that given the opportunity, they will become leaders? Instead of using authority to develop leaders, the church should be looking at leaders who are capable of handling authority.

In light of all the above, the small church should consider a shift in its understanding of leaders and leadership as it moves toward productivity. This shift must be threefold: in its focus, its activity, and its agenda.

First, the church and its leadership must shift their focus from the institution toward the mission. This is a shift from concentrating on *who we are* to *why we are here*. It is easy for the small church to focus on the church as an institution, taking care of its history and values, its property, and its identity. In the natural pattern of a church's life, there comes a point at which shifting values necessitate a focus on the infrastructure of the church to create a sustainable framework for its life: aging buildings need attention and aging persons within the congregation require care. As the church grows and the congregation becomes a family, the natural tendency is to focus on maintaining and strengthening the bonds of relationships, so the attention of the church moves toward providing ministries that are focused on personal growth, on stability, and even on entertainment. If the church is not aware of where it is going, however, the desire to take care of the institution can overwhelm the life of the church to the neglect of its outreach. Without being aware of what is happening, the leaders become like Peter and James, working hard to protect the church against outside threats, seeking to preserve its values for future generations, blind to the work that God is doing outside the walls of the institution they love. Without a new perspective, the church unwittingly dooms itself to demise. The only solution is for Barnabas leadership to move the focus from internal stability to external mission.

Second, the church leadership must shift its activity from administration to management. Administration and management go hand in hand, each essential to the productive church, but there is a clear difference between the two. Administration seeks to organize the church around the proper values, priorities, and procedures, creating the framework for ministry. Administrators set and maintain policies for the proper functioning of the church. As such, administration may be expressed as *"doing the right things."* Good administrative leaders set the agenda for the church through planning and through establishing a vision for the future that expresses the values and mission of the church. They create and maintain order within the leadership through clear lines of authority and accountability. In essence, they define what the church is, establishing and maintaining its identity. Thus, administration is, for the most part, a decision-making enterprise within the leadership of the church and its attention is turned toward the institution. Management, on the other hand, strives to ensure that what the church does is an authentic expression of what the church is and may be expressed as *"doing things right."* As such, it pays attention to how the ministry of the church functions, who carries out the ministry and what results are produced from the work of the church. If administration is primarily decision-oriented, then management is action-oriented. This shift may also be understood as one from the building to the people.

Even though both administration and management are essential to the life and health of the church, in the small church there seems to be a tendency to emphasize administration over management and meetings often reflect this emphasis as leaders invest their time and energy into decisions about finances, building maintenance, and the needs of the church, leaving little time for work on the active ministry of the church. Leaders are often quick to plan what needs to happen, but less anxious to organize how it will happen or who will make it happen. Too often, especially in the small church, the ministry of the church as a whole is actually the collective ministry of individual leaders who carry out their personal mission with little supervision. The church lawn gets mown by a member who lives nearby; shut-ins are visited by friends who make it a part of their weekly routine; children are taught in Sunday school by a retired teacher who loves being with kids. Thank God for these saints, without whom the small church could not exist! But what happens when one gets ill or another has to move away to be near her own children? There is never a decision made to not have Sunday school, but without the dedicated teacher, the program simply fades into oblivion, unless the church leadership becomes intentional about managing the program. A conscientious effort must be made to shift the investment of the leadership away from simply administering the life of the church and toward managing that life in order to grow its ministry.

The final shift that must take place among the leaders in the small church concerns the church's agenda, which is intricately linked to its mission. Definition of the church's agenda comes through asking the question, *"Why are we here?"* Leaders who are willing to struggle with this question enable the church to define its mission and maintain its integrity, yet, too often, this question goes unasked in the small church, the people assuming that the answer is a foregone conclusion. However, true answers that emerge from this struggle are, and perhaps should be, as varied as the churches themselves. Both Barnabas and Peter were effective leaders in the early Church and each would probably have said that they were there to spread the salvation that had been revealed to them in Jesus, yet how that salvation was to be shared was a point of contention between them: Peter saw the agenda focused on protecting and preserving the emerging institution of the Church; Barnabas saw the agenda focused on spreading the kingdom of God. It is in these contrasting perspectives that we can move toward understanding the shift in agenda necessary for the small church.

As churches move through their life cycle there is a natural shift in agenda, reflected in the mission of the church. In the early phase of the church's growth, the agenda is focused on evangelism, on making new disciples to build up the church. As the church matures and becomes more established, the agenda shifts away from making disciples, toward promoting and maintaining the institution, as noted above. While to a certain extent this shift is inevitable, it is unfortunate, redirecting energy, attention, and resources from mission to maintenance. Without clear and intentional redefinition of the agenda, the church is destined to live out the familiar pattern of complacency and decline. Therefore, leaders that are intentional about asking the question of the church's existence help to guide the church toward understanding their agenda and redirecting their energy. Productive leaders keep before them the mandate of making disciples and the mission of the church and help the established church to move from institutional preservation toward dynamic mission. They see the real work of the church taking place in changed lives rather than in institutional recognition, and the church becomes the means for carrying out the mission rather than the result of its success.

The church's agenda may be expressed in a pair of dualities. First, it is both immediate and long term. Flowing out of the church's understanding of mission, it is concerned with the immediate needs of the church in its contemporary setting, seeking to respond to those needs in the best manner possible and shaping its mission to be the most effective expression of its witness. Yet, at the same time, the church must be aware of its larger agenda, what the church must do in the current moment to prepare itself for the future. This duality may also be expressed as the relationship between the local church and the kingdom of God: the local church seeks to respond to the needs of the community in the present, while bringing into its midst a vision of the greater kingdom for future generations. The productive small church integrates its agenda in a manner that utilizes the immediate mission of the church to its community to promote the future kingdom.

Second, it is both foundational and formative, concerning itself with both the mission of the church and the people required to fulfill this mission. A foundational agenda creates the structure required for the church to be in mission; therefore, it moves toward administrative matters as it establishes priorities, maintains order through the establishment of policies and procedures, and attends to the health of the church. All of these are necessary for the church to be in mission. Yet mission does not happen because the church sets priorities and establishes policies: it happens when faithful people live out their faith in the service of the kingdom. Effective leadership also sets an agenda that focuses on people and empowers the members of the church to be in mission. It forms them as disciples so that they can make disciples and attends to their spiritual well-being. Therefore, productive leadership seeks to balance this duality, becoming both foundational and formative.

While creating these shifts in the church, in its focus, activity, and agenda, does not guarantee that its ministry will be productive, without them the small church easily becomes stagnant and un-productive. In and of themselves, these shifts do not fulfill the church's mission, but create the environment in which the people are inspired and motivated to be in mission for the sake of the greater kingdom of God. Leaders that intentionally enter into a dialogue around their reason for existence are enabled to move away from the familiar pattern of the church, creating the potential for the church to enter into a new phase of mission that results in new patterns of vitality.

Setting Out for Deeper Waters

Churches are like living organisms and their life naturally follows a familiar pattern that moves from growth into maintenance and from maintenance into decline. This pattern is echoed in the church's mission, moving from evangelism to Christian care and, eventually, survival. The leadership of the church follows much the same pattern as it begins with great enthusiasm, shifts into a sense of comfort when stability is achieved, then becomes complacent and even burnt out as the church declines. For the small church to recover its productivity, this pattern must be broken, not regressing to the "glory days" of the church but finding a new vision for its future as it seeks to be in ministry with and to its community. This can only happen through the work of its leaders, who are able to shift the church's focus, activity, and agenda. Therefore, it is essential for the church's future to develop leadership that is able to both honor the past and embrace the future and to see itself in service to the greater kingdom of God. Doing this requires productive leaders that embrace certain qualities of character, competence, and contribution.

Growing Leadership

a. Utilizing the demographic data gathered earlier, chart out the church's growth over the last three decades. In your analysis, where does the church fall on the pattern of growth discussed in this chapter?

b. Which of these words best describes the demeanor of your leadership: enthusiastic, comfortable, complacent, bored, burnt out? On what do you base your response? What could you do to recapture the enthusiasm of the church leadership?

c. Analyze how time is spent in church meetings; how much time is spent on issues of administration and how much is spent on management? Is this a healthy balance for the church?

d. Using this chart, make a list of the normal, routine ministry activities of the church, who carries out these activities and how lines of accountability and support for them are maintained.

ACTIVITY	PERSON /GROUP	TO WHOM ARE THEY ACCOUNTABLE?

e. Does this list indicate a healthy, coordinated system of leadership that is well managed? Is it a system that takes the leaders for granted? Is it a haphazard amalgamation of individual leaders to which the church gives little thought? What words would you use to describe the church's leadership style?

8

Characteristics of a Productive Leaders

Abide in me as I abide in you. Just as the branch cannot bear fruit by itself unless it abides in the vine, neither can you unless you abide in me. I am the vine, you are the branches. Those who abide in me and I in them bear much fruit, because apart from me you can do nothing.

—JOHN 15:4–5

MINISTRY IN THE LOCAL church is about making disciples; making disciples is about bearing fruit; Jesus told his disciples that to bear fruit they must remain connected to him. Just as a branch alone cannot bear fruit without the supportive nourishment of the vine itself, the church cannot bear fruit without its leaders, and leaders cannot lead the church to bear fruit without being connected to Jesus. Therefore, the first exploration into the qualities of productive leadership must begin with the characteristics of productive leadership that enable them to establish and maintain their connection to the life-giving, empowering presence of the risen Christ.

In this teaching of Jesus, offered to his disciples as a part of the so-called "farewell discourse" in the Gospel of John—that time when Jesus was preparing his disciples for life and ministry beyond his own death—Jesus gave his intimate followers his greatest words of wisdom so that his ministry would continue through them. That wisdom centered around becoming servants, following his instructions, loving one another, and staying connected. If they did this, they would receive power from the Holy Spirit, bear fruit in their ministry, and find peace and fulfillment in their lives. In these words, then, Jesus began to lay out some of the characteristics necessary for the continued lives of his followers to be able to carry on his work and become productive in their own lives. His insistence that the disciples "abide" in him is the English rendering of the Greek word "*menetei.*" In ancient Greek literature, the word means "*to dwell in,*" understood to be a permanent residence for someone. An extended understanding of the word, and the probable intended use in John's gospel, is "*to remain as one, not to become another or different.*" [1] Hence, the expectation Jesus had for the ongoing lives of the disciples was that they would continue what they had already begun and do so in the same way he himself had been do-ing. Thus, for them to live out their mission was for the work and spirit of Jesus to continue to live through them: they and Jesus would live as one. By extension, then, the qualities Jesus exhibited in his life and work would be those to which the disciples would aspire; they would seek to become "*Christ-like*" in their life and work.

As mentioned previously, through his work at the Lewis Center at Wesley Theological Seminary, Lovett Weems recognizes the first of three categories that identify the qualities of leadership as "character." Perhaps the best understanding of "character" references who one is; that is, one's core values that express her or his identity. As such, to speak of character is to express the qualities of a person that define the priorities of one's life, the principles that guide life itself, and the manner in which a person enters into relationships with others. Character is not a quality that comes and goes, and true character cannot be turned off and on; that is, true character is evident and consistent in one's public and private life, both when people are watching and when one is alone. Thus, character is separate and distinct from behavior, yet it is one's character that gives rise to one's behavior as the guiding principles through which one thinks, decides, and acts. Therefore, Jesus' instructions about "abiding" in him were directed at more than just how the disciples were to act; they pointed to what they were to become in the very core of their being.

Essential Characteristics of Productive Leaders

In writing to the Roman church, Paul described the nature of Christian leaders to which his audience should aspire:

> *Let love be genuine; hate what is evil, hold fast to what is good; love one another with mutual affection; outdo one another in showing*

1. Greek lexicon based on Thayer's and Smith's Bible Dictionary plus others; this is keyed to the large Kittel and the "Theological Dictionary of the New Testament." These files are public domain.

honor. Do not lag in zeal, be ardent in spirit, serve the Lord. Rejoice in hope, be patient in suffering, persevere in prayer. Contribute to the needs of the saints; extend hospitality to strangers.

Romans 12:9–14

Although Paul does not use the language himself, many have referred to this list of Christian characteristics and the spiritual gifts that precede it (vs. 6–8) as "essential" to the life and health of the church; that is, those gifts that make up the essence of the church, without which the church cannot be what it is intended to be. As we consider the leadership of the church that is conducive to productive ministry in our own setting, we also do well to think of the essential characteristics of leaders, those qualities that both make the church what it is called to be and that are consistent with the qualities of character and behavior to which Jesus called his disciples. These are the characteristics that enable leaders to focus their attention on God's vision and bearing fruit for God's kingdom. While consistent with Paul's characteristics, the gifts presented here move toward an understanding that reflects a more contemporary perspective. They guide leaders to both honor the past and the values of the church while addressing the needs of the community. They recognize the importance of the institution of the church as the means by which the people fulfill the mission and ministry of the church. Most of all, they are the qualities of leadership that make disciples. Churches that are productive have leaders that exhibit these characteristics. Churches that lack such leaders fall into patterns of decline and even dysfunction.

In the secular world there is often discussion about "innate," characteristics, qualities that are a part of one's personality. In this sense, they talk about "*natural born leaders*" as though leadership is somehow built into their DNA. From a Christian point of view, however, it is more appropriate to refer to these essential qualities as God-given and the leaders who possess them as those persons whom God raises up to lead God's people. In the Hebrew scriptures we see characters who "receive the Spirit of God" as a gift of empowerment, including the judges, the kings and the prophets. Such language captures the very nature of the act of creation, in which God breathes into Adam the "*ruach*" or "*breath of God*" (which can also be translated as "*spirit*"). It is this understanding that is presumed in the story of Pentecost, when the disciples receive the Holy Spirit, and which Paul brings forward in his many references to the spirit and spiritual gifts.[2] Therefore, as we consider the essential gifts of leadership in the productive church, we understand that these are the gifts that enable leaders to be more like Jesus, more like what God intended humanity to be, and, thus, more in tune with God's vision for the Church. What follows here is a list of those characteristics that this author has observed in productive leaders. While intended to be comprehensive, it is not exhaustive, and this list may most certainly be expanded to include other characteristics or variations of those listed that are essential to given churches. It is, therefore, best considered as the beginning of such a list rather than the completion thereof.

First and foremost, productive leaders are *always spiritual*. To be "spiritual," in this sense, means to be aware of the presence and influence of God's spirit, also expressed as the spirit of the risen Christ and the Holy Spirit. For productive leaders, this is not an occasional awareness, but a constant one. They do not place their spirituality on a shelf, to be referenced sporadically as the situation demands, but bring their awareness of God's presence into every thought, decision, action, and relationship. A few decades ago, there was a craze running through the world of Christian young adults referred to as the WWJD movement: *"What Would Jesus Do?"* The idea was to use this question to make difficult decisions in life, imaging the example of Christ to guide that decision. Truly, this *is* the understood authority for the life of all Christians: bringing the example of Christ to bear on life's toughest moments. To be always spiritual, however, means that the example of Christ becomes the motivating factor in all of life, not just in the moments of difficult decisions. In this sense, productive leaders begin to approach the fullness of Christ's love for God and neighbor in all they do, a process that John Wesley called *"going on to perfection."* Productive leaders are constantly aware of the fact that for them to live is for Christ to live through them, as spoken of by the Apostle Paul.[3]

Also, the spirituality of productive leaders is intentional. They do not sit idly by, waiting for the moment of the spirit's arrival, but actively, even aggressively, seek out the presence of God. They engage in communal activities that place them in God's presence, especially worship, fellowship, and education. These leaders also engage in many of the private spiritual disciplines, including prayer, fasting, meditation, and Bible study. They are purposeful in their lives of faith, seeking to be good stewards of their

2. (see Romans 12 and I Corinthians 12 as examples).

3. (see Philippians 1:21)

time and talents as well as their resources. Many would refer to productive leaders as "people of faith" because they bring their faith understanding to bear throughout their lives and seek out opportunities to grow that faith. However, their faith is more than a belief system: it permeates all of their decision making for sure, but it also becomes a motivating factor in their lifestyle and relationships as well. In this sense, they bring into reality the words of James: *"Show me your faith apart from your works, and I by my works will show you my faith."*[4]

Productive leaders are *visionary*: they look to the future and plan where they want to be. Speaking of leadership, Patrick Atkinson has said:

> *The single most important quality for a leader is vision. Where do you want your cause to end up? In other words, where do you want to take the people you are leading? Suppose I was standing in the middle of a crowded room and suddenly I jumped up and said, "Let's go!" or "Follow me." People would look at me and say, "Who is this guy and where is he going?"*
>
> *In this situation, people might start laughing at me, but they definitely wouldn't run in circles with me. Yet this is exactly what is happening in corporate boardrooms across America today. Businesses and entire nations are being led by people who have no clear plan, no vision of where they are going or how they want to get there. The number one trait good leaders have is a clear vision of where they want their group to go.*[5]

Placed in the context of productive leadership, vision—more particularly God's vision—becomes the driving force in those leaders that are most effective. Their faith gives shape to the preferred reality of God's kingdom in their midst and their deepest desires are to make this vision a reality. In several of the stories already noted in these pages one can see how leaders worked to make the possibilities of the future the realities of their current lives. This is exactly what productive leaders do as they are guided through discernment to understand their vision and motivated by faith to bring that vision into reality. Thus, a part of being visionary is also the gift of discernment, the ability to see through the challenges of human desire and strife to comprehend the vision of God's kingdom. Like Amos, Hosea and the other prophets, productive leaders are able to understand the human condition

---

4. James 2:18b

5. *Leadership Defined.* Insight Publishing Company, 2005, pp.33–50. Interviews conducted by: David E. Wright, President, International Speakers Network.

and see new possibilities and opportunities that lie beyond the human imagination and inclination, then to motivate others to join them in the quest for a greater reality beyond the brokenness that results from Sin.

Productive leaders are *servants*. When Jesus gathered his disciples for his final farewell, the first thing he did was to kneel before them and wash their feet. Having finished the task, he asked them:

> *Do you know what I have done to you? You call me Teacher and Lord—and you are right, for that is what I am. So if I, your Lord and Teacher, have washed your feet, you also ought to wash one another's feet. For I have set you an example, that you also should do as I have done to you.*[6]

Clearly, Jesus placed a high priority on servanthood, often referencing the role of a servant as the highest quality of being a disciple. [7] Just as it was in the world of Jesus, placing servanthood as a quality of leadership is both a role-reversal and a bit anathema to current leaders. Today's trend is to see leaders out front, boldly proclaiming the truth that they understand and guiding others in what to do while seeing the menial tasks of daily chores as the lot of lesser persons. Yet consider some of the great leaders of the world, people like Mother Theresa and Mahatma Ghandi, who literally changed the face of humanity for large groups of poor people by taking on the role of a servant. True leaders turn their attention outward, understanding their leadership to be about changing the lives of others, not about power or prestige. They lead by example, showing others the path to fulfillment by walking ahead of them down that path, placing the needs of others before their own needs, a practice identified as "hospitality" in the Bible and listed as one of the essential characteristics by the Apostle Paul. Others are willing to follow these persons because they can see themselves in the actions of these leaders and observe the fulfillment that serving others brings them.

Yet it is clear, from the Biblical perspective, that servanthood is not to be understood as a demeaning or debasing characteristic, but one of honor and respect. Jesus made the point quite clearly: *"whoever wishes to be great among you must be your servant . . ."*[8] Leaders who choose service as their means of expression in ministry do so out of respect for the needs of others and in imitation of the one whom they follow. In the productive church, the most effective leaders are not those who tell others what to do; they are the

6. John 13:12b–15

7. (see Luke 22:26 or Matthew 23:11)

8. Matthew 20:26

ones who, through their actions and attitudes, show others what to do, how to do it, and the rewards of being in ministry. They do not separate themselves from the people of the church and community but see themselves as a part of the lives of those they seek to lead. In the words of Martin Luther King Jr. they understand that:

> In a real sense all life is inter-related. All men are caught in an inescapable network of mutuality, tied in a single garment of destiny. Whatever affects one directly, affects all indirectly. I can never be what I ought to be until you are what you ought to be, and you can never be what you ought to be until I am what I ought to be . . .[9]

Thus, they see their own future fulfilled in the lives of those that they seek to serve, and the people of the church are willing to follow them precisely for that reason: they know the desire of the leaders is not self-fulfillment, but the betterment of all. These leaders are willing to take on whatever tasks are necessary for the fulfillment of the vision to which they hold, knowing that it is in working toward the kingdom that they are best able to participate in it. Furthermore, all this is in response to grace, that free gift of love that they know is the reason for the Church to begin with. The end result is a productive church: "If you want to thrive, serve . . ."[10]

Productive leaders are *disciples*. What is a disciple? One who follows. More precisely, a disciple is one devoted to the leadership of another, to replicating their actions and to learning from their understanding. Productive leaders are themselves followers and they are effective in their leadership precisely for this reason. Others follow them because they are able to understand the dynamics of being a follower and identify with those they seek to lead. Just as the twelve disciples sought to honor Jesus in their lives, true and effective leaders of the church model their leadership after the example of Christ, identifying with his character, his priorities, and his ministry. Thus, they honor the authority of the one they seek to follow.

Beyond the authority of Jesus, however, truly productive leaders are able to recognize, accept, and honor authority from other sources as well. They recognize the authority of their denominational theology, doctrine and polity and seek to honor the traditions of their larger Church. They are cognizant of and appreciate the traditions and values of their local church.

9. Martin Luther King Jr., *"Letter from Birmingham Jail: Martin Luther King Jr.'s Letter from Birmingham Jail and the Struggle That Changed a Nation"* © 2019 Goodreads, Inc. Mobile version

10. Weems, *Leadership in the Wesleyan Spirit*, p. 40

They also accept that their leadership combines with that of others to make the church what it can be; sometimes they lead other leaders; sometimes they follow the lead of those whom they trust. Lovett Weems dispels the myth that some people are leaders and some are followers:

> *The reality is that all are leaders and all are followers. The genius is to know when to be which. In the course of any day, all of us are constantly going back and forth between being one and being the other.*[11]

Understood in this way, productive leadership is an exercise in power sharing, knowing that individual leadership is amplified, not diminished, in the presence of other leaders, provided that all are working toward the fulfillment of a shared vision.

Productive leaders are *committed*. In the fast-paced world in which we live, commitment is a virtue that is sometimes hard to find. The tendency that so often prevails, whether in church, in business, or in pleasure, is to focus on a project or idea as long as it meets our needs and expectations or as long as it is enjoyable. Rampant consumerism has created within the American culture the idea that the life span of everything is limited, so you only need hold on to it until it breaks or no longer meets your desires. The rapid rise and fall of independent churches and fellowships speaks to the extent to which this same philosophy has carried over into the world of religion. Instead of working through disagreements and challenges, disgruntled church members simply break away and form their own new community that does not produce the challenges and struggles that make them discontented. Once a non-existent category in America, *"no religious preference"* has now become a dominant answer on many religious surveys. All this bodes ill for committed leadership.

The number one cause of failure is giving up too soon. Especially in the world of small business, the idea may be great, but, whether due to a lack of financial capital or ebbing enthusiasm, many businesses fail within the first year. In the same way many church ministries fail because they are inadequately funded or because the commitment of the leadership wains in the midst of challenges. Productive leaders are dedicated to their vision and work through the obstacles before them rather than giving up. We would do well to understand the commitment of leadership—and the

---

11. Weems, *Leadership in the Wesleyan Spirit*, p. 67.

entire Christian faith, for that matter—in light of the marriage vow: *". . . for better, for worse; for richer or poorer; in sickness and in health . . ."*

Productive leaders are *passionate*. One of the essential characteristics listed by Paul, the apostle expresses this trait as *"zeal."* The words passion and zeal both speak to strong belief in one's commitments. We often associate both of these words with people who are effusive in their description of what they are doing, who love to tell their story so that others can share in their enthusiasm. Productive leaders believe that the ministry of the church makes a difference and are quick to invite others to join them. The most effective leaders derive their passion from knowing that they are a part of something larger than themselves, having given of themselves for the greater kingdom of God and are, thus, proud to share the good news of what God is doing through them.

Likewise, productive leaders are *compassionate*. Their zeal for ministry is not expressed for processes or procedures, but for people. They focus their attention on the lives that are changed for the sake of the kingdom and for the betterment of those people whose needs are being met. The New Testament closely links compassion with the word *"pity,"* offering each as an acceptable translation of the Greek, but there is a difference: *"pity"* implies a feeling of sorrow for the plight of others; *"compassion"* is *"sympathetic consciousness of others' distress together with a desire to alleviate it."*[12] Leaders express pity when they extend the resources of the church to help others—ministry *"to"* the people; compassionate leaders stand with others in the midst of their struggles, journeying with them as together they work to alleviate suffering and need—ministry *"with"* the people. Thus, compassionate leaders are involved in the lives of those with whom they are in ministry, passionate about the work that God is doing in their lives, and committed to expressing the fullness of God's love to all.

Productive leaders are *authentic*. Much has been written about authenticity in recent years and the need for leaders to be real. This characteristic is often expressed through words like *"transparent,"* *"genuine"* and *"honest."* In more common vernacular, with authentic leaders, *"what you see is what you get,"* expressing the feeling that there is no sense of duplicity and there are no hidden agendas. People know where authentic leaders stand and that for which they stand. From the perspective of faith, *"authenticity"* might be better expressed with the word *"integrity."* Productive leaders have integrated their beliefs with their actions, becoming, in the words of the

---

12. Merriam-Webster Online Dictionary. © 2019 Merriam-Webster, Incorporated.

author of James, *". . . doers of the word, and not merely hearers who deceive themselves."*[13] Their faith is not a simple set of principles or a group of ideas to which they ascribe, but the framework around which their life is built and the standard by which they engage in all that they do. Thus, they can be trusted to act in their best understanding of the mandates of the Gospel, even by those who may disagree with that particular understanding.

Furthermore, the integrity of productive leaders extends beyond their leadership in the church into all aspects of their lives. Their focus is not only on leading the church, but also on leading people as an expression of both their compassion for those people and a love for the kingdom of God. There is no separation between their religious life and their secular life, just as God does not separate the two: as God's concern is for the wholeness of life, so is that of the productive leader.

Productive leaders are *humble*. They clearly understand that ministry is not about them and their success, but about the kingdom and its fulfill-ment in the world. Thus, ministry turns from an understanding that places them in charge, wherein their own abilities bring about success, toward an understanding that what they do and what they are able to accomplish is a gift of God's grace, as God empowers and enables them for the task of ministry. When the late, great Methodist theologian Albert Outler had the opportunity to comment on the role of ministers as shepherds, he replied, *"O no, we are not shepherds . . . we are only sheepdogs listening for the voice of the one, true shepherd."*[14] This sense of humility permeated Dr. Outler's life and is a model for all who would seek to be productive leaders: we are not the ones in charge and we are not the ones who decide what is best for the church; we are merely the agents of God's action, the conduit of God's grace, and while God certainly has raised us up to be leaders, God's Church survived for twenty centuries without us and will likely continue for quite some time after we are gone. We do not bring about the kingdom of God; we simply point to it through our leadership and invite others to join us as we journey toward it.

Functional Characteristics of Productive Leaders

The above list of essential characteristics forms a foundation for the con-sideration of productive leadership in the church and seeks to link the

13. James 1:22

14. From a private conversation with Dr. Outler and this author in February 1974.

qualities of leadership necessary for the church today with those set forth by the apostle Paul in his world. However, it does not exhaust the qualities of leadership that enable the church to be productive. There is a second list that should be considered, one that grows out of the world of leadership in general, characteristics that might well be seen in the world of business, education, and industry. These are termed "functional" for the sake of this discussion, since they enable leadership in the church to function in a more productive manner. While the essential characteristics maintain a sense of integrity with the Christian faith and traditions, functional characteristics open the door for managing relationships and often form a bridge between character and competence. Whereas the church struggles to be authentic without the essential characteristics, it can survive and even thrive without functional characteristics; yet the quality of the church's life and ministry is, nevertheless, enhanced in their presence. Therefore, having been observed in the leaders of productive churches, this list of functional characteristics is offered as those qualities that, combined with the essential characteristics, enable leaders to become more effective and, thereby, more productive.

Productive leaders are *curious*. Curious persons seek to know more, asking questions and finding answers, delving into the less obvious, uncovering that which is hidden to the eyes and understanding of others. They are eager to learn, excited about the possibilities that greater knowledge and understanding might bring. In this sense, they are invested in hope: the possibilities for the future that have yet to be revealed. Therefore, they are willing and eager to ask questions, both in their personal quest for additional information and in their relationships with others, knowing that the next piece of data, the next tidbit of insight might bring a new world of possibilities to them and the ministry of the church. Productive leaders use their curiosity to move beyond the norms with which they are surrounded, shifting out of the reality of *"what is"* to the potential of *"what might be,"* and seldom fall into the trap of resisting change to maintain the status quo, never falling back to the trite phrase *". . . but we've never done it that way before . . ."* This sense of curiosity keeps the church moving in a positive direction, exploring new concepts, new perspectives, and new opportunities in the quest for what God might have in store for their ministry. It is also a natural component of discernment, leading them to clarity in the vision that God shares with them and the church.

Productive leaders are *active listeners,* which is a natural complement to curiosity. Listening is an art that requires practice and is evidence of the character of the leader who desires to understand the expressions, ideas, and feelings of others. Rather than shape the conversation through their own words, productive leaders regard conversations as an opportunity to engage in relationships, whether with individuals or in group settings. Therefore, their conversations are shaped in response to those around them, building a system of ideas in a collaborative spirit. Rather than use the time others are speaking to shape their next expressions, active listeners hear, process, and digest the words of others to move the conversation to a true dialogue instead of a stream of individual monologues. A by-product of active listening is that such leaders honor others and value their ideas, even if they do not necessarily agree with them.

Productive leaders are *self-assured, but not arrogant.* Leaders who are self-assured elicit feelings of confidence and respect from those that seek to follow them; leaders who are arrogant breed uncertainty and suspicion. This quality of self-assurance is a product of faith: belief in one's abilities certainly, but also trust in the ability of God's guidance and the equipping nature of the Holy Spirit. Arrogance, on the other hand, comes from trusting too much in one's own abilities. While arrogance places one above others in efforts of self-promotion, self-confidence allows leaders to regard others as having something valuable to contribute. Therefore, self-confident leaders honor those around them and work to bring out the best qualities of those they seek to lead, empowering them to be their best in the knowledge that God's Kingdom is best served by what they do together. Arrogant leaders, however, diminish the service of others, threatened when they rise to recognition, unable to accept the value of their contributions for fear of losing their own sense of value. Leaders who are self-assured become productive in their ministry; arrogant leaders become destructive, because they are a hinderance to a sense of collaboration.

Productive leaders are *courageous.* Motivated by their self-assurance, productive leaders are willing to step forward when others hold back because they are not threatened by the fear of rejection. Since they believe that their greatest worth comes from being a servant of God, they understand that their ultimate ambition is not to be praised by others, but to use their leadership to honor God. Therefore, productive leaders are willing to take risks in order to guide others toward the fulfillment of God's Kingdom, knowing that this is the highest goal toward which they can strive. While others might make decisions based on the fear of failure, productive leaders are motivated by the possibilities of success in ministry that God will make possible through their willingness to stand up for what they understand to be God's leading. Their courage enables leaders to move the ministry of the church into new avenues of service that reach beyond the norm and they are willing and able to promote these new opportunities as ways in which the Kingdom of God may be brought into the lives of those around them, in their church and in their community.

Productive leaders are *tenacious*. Consider the image of a person holding on for dear life over the edge of a cliff: the future depends on the strength of the grip. Often the future of the small church is determined by the strength of the leaders' grip, those unwilling to give up on a hopeful future because of the realities of the present. But productive leaders are not always the ones hanging off the edge: sometimes they are the ones extending their helping hand from the sure footing of the world above the cliff, unwilling to let go of the ministry of the church and let it fall into oblivion. Yet this tenacity does not emerge out of a sense of blind or prideful stubbornness, like a farmer unwilling to plow up the fields of the past because they once produced a crop; it comes from the hopefulness of the leader who knows that the seeds planted will yet grow, who waters and cultivates the field knowing that God's spirit will bring them to life. Thus, tenacity is a by-product of the commitment to making disciples identified above. Productive leaders are not swayed by evidence of early defeat, willing to give up on ministry because it has not yet found its strength, but motivated and encouraged to keep working, knowing that in the midst of faithful commitment God will bring forth a harvest.

However, while productive leaders are both courageous and tenacious, they are also *flexible*. They are active listeners who hear others and appreciate the leadership they have to offer, and they are not so arrogant that they believe that their way is the only way. Their commitment is not to their own idea or way of doing things, but to the fulfillment of God's vision and God's kingdom. History often credits Henry Ford with the creation of the assembly line, but this is a myth: the assembly line existed long before the Ford Motor Company was born. Ford was committed to making an automobile that could be afforded by the average household in America and by applying the assembly line model of manufacturing he was able to reach his goal. Flexibility in leadership comes from discerning God's vision for ministry and using whatever appropriate means are available to bring that vision into reality; if current strategies are not working to that end, productive leaders are able and willing to adjust the strategy for ministry to achieve their goals, just as Ford brought a new process to the world of making cars.

This sense of flexibility grows out of a concern for people and the context in which they live, not out of a self-serving personality that seeks to promote one's ideas or even one's expertise. Effective leadership is not born in oneself, but in the people. Thus, productive leaders shape their vision around the people and their needs and are willing to adapt their strategies based on what they believe is needed to live out the kingdom of God in the midst of those people. Furthermore, they are able to use whatever style of leadership is required to meet those needs at a given time. While placing a priority on the needs of the people by its very nature calls forth a collaborative process in leadership, truly effective leaders are able to shift to a more authoritarian style as mandated by the context and immediacy of the needs, not as an exercise in domination and control, but as the most appropriate strategy to achieve the church's vision.

Developing Productive Leadership

Although we affirm the givenness of leadership characteristics, we must also acknowledge that once given, it is up to the individual leader to grow in those attributes that bring productivity. Like the muscles of the human body, increased use and activity of these characteristics allows them to grow and become stronger. It is, therefore, incumbent upon each leader to first identify his or her gifts, then work to expand and strengthen those gifts to grow in leadership. To this end, the reader will find a helpful exercise in appendix B, which encourages one to honestly assess the personal leadership characteristics identified above. Responsible use of this assessment identifies areas of potential strength and guides the reader to work toward growing in these characteristics as a means of moving toward more productive leadership. This exercise may also be downloaded from the website *Productive Discipleship*: www.productivediscipleship.com

9

Competencies of a Productive Leaders

Now there are varieties of gifts, but the same Spirit; and there are varieties of services, but the same Lord; and there are varieties of activities, but it is the same God who activates all of them in everyone. To each is given the manifestation of the Spirit for the common good. To one is given through the Spirit the utterance of wisdom, and to another the utterance of knowledge according to the same Spirit, to another faith by the same Spirit, to another gifts of healing by the one Spirit, to another the working of miracles, to another prophecy, to another the discernment of spirits, to another various kinds of tongues, to another the interpretation of tongues. All these are activated by one and the same Spirit, who allots to each one individually just as the Spirit chooses.

For just as the body is one and has many members, and all the members of the body, though many, are one body, so it is with Christ.

—I CORINTHIANS 12:4–12

IN THE TWELFTH CHAPTER of I Corinthians, Paul turns his attention to spiritual gifts, the responsibilities of individual members of the church, and how the church, as the Body of Christ, works together. This iconic image needs little explanation, save that responsibility for the church rests on every person and that God raises up each person to use his or her gifts in the best and most efficient way so that the Body of Christ may be full-functioning and effective. Persons are called to identify, refine, and implement the gifts they have, knowing that the Body of Christ is dependent on them. This is the first step for serving in and becoming leaders of the church. But Paul moves beyond his focus on the individual to point out that, beyond the self-improvement of personal refinement, responsible stewards of God's gifts must learn how to use their gifts in relation to others, integrate their gifts into the total life of the church—the Body of Christ—and supportively appreciate the gifts of others. Just as the body cannot be fully functional without all its members working together, the church cannot be complete without the shared abilities of all its members. Just as the absence of one part of the body does not necessarily render the body useless . . . the loss of a finger, for instance . . . the absence of leadership from a single member does not render the church ineffective; but it does place a larger burden on the remaining members of the church and increases the difficulty in the church's implementation of its ministries. Conversely, when all the parts of the body work cooperatively, the body is able to accomplish extraordinary things and when all of the members of the church are willing and able to contribute their unique set of skills, with shared responsibility and mutual appreciation, the ministries of the church can reach extraordinary heights. In this understanding is the framework for considering the competencies of productive leaders.

In the previous chapter, the word "character" was used to express the qualities of a person that define the priorities of one's life, the principles that guide life itself, and the way a person enters into relationships with others. As such, "character" refers to *who a person is*, the core of one's being and the values of one's life. "Competency" on the other hand is *what a person does*. It refers to the ability to perform a task in an efficient and successful way, thus references the skills and abilities of the individual, including the knowledge of how to use those skills. Yet the word also points beyond the skills themselves, implying that the use of the skills brings about some sense of success or accomplishment. Thus, for the purposes of understanding the competencies of productive leaders, the word is here used to name the qualities of a leader who exercises authority, guidance, and service to the church. While character is best understood as a gift of God's grace, competencies may be both given and acquired. Whether a gift or an acquired skill, however, competencies are improved by diligent application and practice, just as the body is built up through exercise and conditioning. More importantly, they are the way in which the leader's character becomes manifest in service, activity, and relationships. Truly productive leaders learn how to integrate character and competence, enabling the things they do and the skills they use to be an expression of their character and to bear fruit for the Kingdom.

It is worth noting here that this discussion of competencies focuses on the general leadership of the church and not specific functions within the church. In the twelfth chapter of Romans (as noted previously) Paul identifies seven spiritual gifts, some of which may be considered as competencies. In several other places, including I Corinthians 12, he sets forth similar lists of gifts that might be considered in the same way. These lists include such things as preaching, teaching, giving, and so forth, gifts with which God endows people so that they may provide what is necessary for the church at a particular time. The efficacy of these gifts depends on individuals applying their talents to the ministry of the church, performing specific functions within the greater ministry of the church. While these gifts most certainly fall into the category of "competencies," they are, by nature, very individualistic. Many of these gifts, therefore, move toward a sense of vocational ministry, so we often refer to persons as "teachers" or "preachers" or "prophets" as descriptors of their role within the institution of the church. They are in and of themselves a set of skills that are essential for the church and the proficient use of these skills reflects competency, but the use itself does not necessarily imply productive leadership. So, for the purposes of considering leadership in the church, they are not included in this discussion so that we may focus our attention on those skills that are turned toward the shared ministry of the church.

In considering the skills common to productive leaders, it must be noted that, like spiritual gifts, the skills evidenced by productive leaders vary by individual, just as Paul affirms. Not all leaders excel in all the skills and each local church has its own unique needs that require skills distinct to its setting. Particular skills necessary in one church may not be required in another and skills that help one church grow and thrive may be unproductive in a different setting. Productive leaders are able to discern the ministry needs in their unique context and call forth the skills required for that ministry, either their own or the skills of those with whom they serve. However, there are some skills that manifest themselves repeatedly in local churches that seem to lead the church toward productive ministry, and those are the skills identified here.

In considering the competencies inherent in productive leaders, it is important to view them from three perspectives. First, competencies related to the uniqueness of the church; second, competencies related to managing others; third, competencies that integrate the abilities of the leaders with the unique needs of the church.

Competencies for Leadership in the Church

Productive leaders are able to evaluate the church and its ministry in a critical manner and bring forth from themselves the competencies they deem necessary in a given moment of time. These qualities of leadership may vary over the life of the leader as both the church and person mature in their relationship with one another. They are contextual in nature and depend on both knowledge and discernment for their application. Leaders who manifest these competencies both know and value the uniqueness of their local church and seek to use the character of the church to grow ministry for the Kingdom.

First and foremost, *productive leaders are able to keep before themselves and the church its vision and derive their guidance and inspiration from that vision.* The importance of a sense of vision for the church has been discussed previously and is the single most important factor in enabling a church to be productive through its leadership. Furthermore, this vision is not based solely on the values of the church nor on the needs of the community, but on God's desire for the church to be in ministry in a particular way to a particular group of people and productivity is measured by the extent to which the church is able to use the God-given abilities within the congregation to make disciples among these persons. Productive leaders understand all this and in all matters of decision-making and implementation place God's vision before themselves, their own dreams, and their personal desires. They are able to do this through an understanding of the local church as but one piece of the greater kingdom of God, a sense of connectedness with others who are also working for the fulfillment of God's vision for the world and the Church. This focus on connectionalism draws its meaning from the image of the body Paul uses to call people to responsible work and relationships within the local church. Thus, leaders see their church as a small, but essential, part of the larger Body of Christ: without them the greater Body cannot be whole; with them, the greater body is able to thrive. Their ministry, therefore, enables the greater Church to grow and the kingdom itself to become more discernibly present in the life of their community and in the global community as well.

Second, *productive leaders understand their leadership to be a dynamic enterprise.* Productive leaders understand that each day is a time of new beginnings that brings forward a new hope as God makes all things new. The love of God is moving ever onward and the hope that is taught by their faith brings them to embrace the newness that God brings. In this newness, they understand that God is far more interested in what the church will become than in what the church has been. This means that they are always open to change, not as a means of discarding the past, but as a way of honoring it and bringing it into the future and into the new potential that God is forever creating. Therefore, they live into this hope by constantly embracing the possibilities of the future and they are able to shift their leadership as these possibilities arise. They are able to assess the needs required of them and adjust what they offer to meet those needs in an effective and appropriate way. They themselves work to improve their leadership, allowing their skills and abilities to grow with the vision of the church. Like the captain of a sailboat, they are able to adjust the sails of their leadership to suit the winds of God's Spirit that are blowing. Doing this allows them to stay focused on their priorities and place the vision of the church above their own ego and expertise, using the energy of God's spirit to drive the life and ministry of the church.

Third, *productive leaders are able to understand and appreciate the culture of the church.* Every local church has its own, unique culture. That culture is derived from years and decades of the people living together, working together, suffering together, and rejoicing together. Its culture represents the amalgamation of all the things that make that church what it is and the values that they hold dear. Without their culture, the church has no identity and any threat to that culture brings a danger of losing their identity. Productive leaders understand this and learn to appreciate the culture of their church, even though they may disagree with the character and importance of some of its elements. Thus, productive leaders know how to identify the cultural values that underlie the decisions and actions of the people of the church and then, in turn, use those values to move the church forward toward its vision. In doing so, they are skilled in sharing their appreciation for the accumulated values of the church and, especially, the people and events that have given rise to those values over time. They lift them up and use their example as a source of inspiration, but do not dwell on them in a nostalgic manner, creating a longing for what has been. Rather, they draw inspiration from the past leadership, motivating persons to move into the future. Just as past saints rose to meet the challenges before the church, calling forth and naming the values of the culture they created enables productive leaders to inspire future leaders to the same sense of service and commitment.

But what if the cultural values of the church are detrimental or, worse, counter-productive to the church's ability to fulfill its vision? Clearly, they must be changed in order for the church to move forward, but as shown in the example of "Seeing Church" in Chapter 1, abrupt and aggressive change that does not honor the existing culture and values of the church is equally damaging. Is it possible to honor the values and set them aside at the same time? The answer is *"yes,"* but doing so requires a great amount of skill, knowing how to appreciate others for their leadership while also looking toward the future vision of the church. Dismissing or demeaning past leaders and the values they established is not in the spirit of the Body of Christ set forth by the Apostle Paul and denies a sense of Christian love; finding their positive attributes and lifting them up *is*, and productive leaders are able to do this. Therefore, a part of the competency of effective leadership includes seeing the best in others, appreciating their values, and working toward an appreciation for the differences on which the church can build its future.

Competencies for Leading Leaders

Leading others requires abilities that grow out of relationships and focuses on shared leadership. The competencies necessary for this ability are based on the recognition of both the character and abilities of others and place value on what others have to offer in the ministry of the church. Generally speaking, these competencies reflect an appreciation for others and the leadership that they offer, both in the past and in the present moment of the life of the local church. Furthermore, they grow out of a sense of connectionalism and mutual support, knowing that the ministry of the church is the synergy of the ministry of all its members and that the church can be productive only when the members themselves move toward productivity.

Consider for a moment the image of a symphony orchestra. This orchestra consists of multiple sections of instruments, each of which produces a unique sound. Within each section, there are multiple players, each playing a unique set of notes. These notes are from a score, composed to create the music itself. All these notes and the sound from all these instruments combine to create a harmony that is sometimes simple, sometimes complex, but always intended to produce the sound envisioned by the composer. Shift this image to the ministry of the church: God is the composer; the church's vision is the score; the members of the church are the players.

Yet to bring all this together, a conductor is necessary, keeping the players focused on the score, listening to the sounds produced, lifting up certain instruments to accent their sounds at the proper moment, blending each element into a harmonious whole. Imagine the cacophony of each player deciding on the notes to play without such a score, or that of a church that has no vision. Imagine the sound of an orchestra with only one type of instrument, or a church that has only one type of ministry: monotonous and un-interesting. Imagine if the whole orchestra played only the same note together, or a church focused on a single issue: forceful but lacking the complexity that adds the beauty to the performance. The effective church's conductor is a productive leader and the skills required of these leaders are little different from those of a skillful orchestra leader.

Therefore, productive church members are grown when leaders *share power and responsibility.* These leaders understand that the strength of the church is in the laity and that productivity grows with diversity. Just as the harmony of a symphony is dependent upon the multiplicity of the instruments, the local church finds its beauty in the diversity of its members and the unique character, skills, and abilities that they bring to the life of the church. Productive leaders affirm that the total leadership of the church is an amalgamation of the uniqueness of each individual. They also know that each individual, themselves included, is limited in the abilities she or he possesses, but the aggregate abilities of the church expands exponentially when leaders combine their efforts and abilities. Therefore, they not only accept, but welcome and seek out the leadership of others, knowing that the productivity of the church is enhanced in the combination of the skills of each person. Their style of leadership moves away from an authoritarian perspective and toward a conciliar one as they utilize the uniqueness of individual leaders to create a productive ministry that approaches a sense of wholeness. Rather than feel threatened by others and the values and competencies that they bring to the ministry of the church, productive leaders know that their own competencies are enhanced when combined with those of others and they seek to create a sense of mutuality and respect within the total leadership that binds persons together with bonds of respect and appreciation.

Working in this spirit, productive leaders willingly delegate responsibility and leadership to others, knowing that the strength of the whole church is increased with the diversity of leadership. Their trust and confidence in others are displayed in their willingness to share the power of leadership rather than hoard that power for themselves, both allowing and encouraging other leaders to share in the responsibility for the direction and outcome of the church's ministry. There is, however, a fine line between "delegation" and "relegation." One who delegates assigns tasks to others while maintaining a sense of responsibility for the outcome of the task or decision, establishing lines of accountability and support in the completion of the task without micro-managing the other person's work. One who relegates gives up responsibility for the task or decision, leaving the other person to bear the consequences, for good or ill. Delegators trust others and work with them, valuing the importance of the task or decision given; relegators absolve themselves of responsibility and distance themselves from those that they lead.

Furthermore, productive leaders understand that sharing responsibilities is not only beneficial to the church and its ministry: it also has positive consequences in the lives of those with whom power is shared. Such persons are affirmed in their worth and given the opportunity to expand their own discipleship, which in turn provides experience and maturity that contributes to their own productivity. Sharing leadership with others is not merely an administrative strategy to expand leadership, it is also a pastoral expression that grows disciples. Therefore, good leaders are pleased to share responsibility with others, even though it is sometimes easier to perform certain tasks alone, knowing that this, too, is an exercise in making disciples.

In working with others, productive leaders *provide resources necessary for the other leaders to do their work.* Leadership is more than pointing the way for others to go. True leadership includes bearing a sense of responsibility for those being led. In the local church it means that, out of a sense of mutual respect, effective leaders know and understand that the complete ministry of the church depends on the full functioning of each of its leaders and that the ministries of the church can never reach their full potential without all of the members and leaders reaching their full potential. Out of this sense of responsibility, therefore, productive leaders ensure that resources are available that enable the full functioning of each of their fellow leaders as well as the entirety of the church family. At a programmatic level, this means adequate provision of physical space, financial resources, and personnel, working with other bodies and committees within the church to ensure these resources are available as needed, moving toward the fulfillment of the church's vision. At a practical level, it means being prepared and anticipating the requirements for productive leadership. Simple matters of providing clear and concise agendas, informational materials, action plans, and financial statements are an absolute necessity for meetings, to make the most efficient use of their time. Productive leaders are able and willing to anticipate these needs and work to ensure that these resources are available to others in order to empower them to participate at the highest level in the work of the committee or task force within the church. It may also mean the same sense of anticipation in the scheduling of meetings, both in terms of time and location, allowing the greatest range of participation by others. In all of this, productive leaders focus their attention on the desired outcome of the meeting, not on personal agendas, working to fulfill the purpose of the gathering in order to move toward the fulfillment of the church's vision.

Closely related to the provision of resources, productive leaders *communicate clearly, consistently, and effectively.* For leaders to provide leadership, they must know what is happening and be prepared to share in the responsibilities called for. Productive leaders ensure that those they are leading are informed in a manner that helps them prepare for their work and are updated regarding the progress of the tasks at hand. Regular, honest, and transparent communications facilitate this sharing of information and progress and they may take the form of official communications in print or by electronic means, or as informal conversations at a personal or small group level. They also ensure that decisions of the committee or task group are clear, understood, and recorded for future reference, whether in formal minutes of the meeting or in some form of record available to others (beyond personal notes for one's own benefit). Communications with others are not taken for granted but are an intentional focus of effective leaders and productive leaders are always seeking to improve the level of communications with others.

Finally, productive leaders *honor the work of others.* Knowing that the strength of the church's ministry rests in the diversity of the Body of Christ and that they bear a sense of responsibility for the full functioning of that body, good leaders maintain a personal appreciation for the work that others do and are quick to affirm that work. Their affirmation is both private and public. In private, this gratitude may be expressed as a thank-you note, a personal conversation, or a simple expression of "well done." In public, it may be a formal recognition of individual contributions or the collective work of the group. It may also take the form of attributing the origin of ideas to the responsible individuals or the affirmation of specific contributions to the task. In all these cases, the expressed gratitude of the productive leader is authentic, honest, sincere, and heartfelt. On the opposite side of this competency, productive leaders never take the work, participation, and contributions of others for granted: even minor efforts are acknowledged and celebrated as a significant contribution toward the fulfillment of the church's vision.

Competencies for Integrating the Church and its Leaders

The third group of competencies relates to the integration of the abilities of the leaders with the needs of the church and forms a bridge between the other two sets of competencies, combining the awareness of the needs and values of the church with interpersonal relationships, thereby allowing a person to lead others into effective and productive service in the church. The bridge that they build is between the other people in the church, knowing and acknowledging the gifts that they bring to the church's ministry, and the needs of the church, all guided by the church's vision.

Productive leaders *work to build an effective team.* A good example of this sense of team building can be seen in Acts 6, wherein the Apostles, overburdened with the mounting responsibilities for the emerging community of Christians, realize that they are incapable of meeting the needs of this community by themselves.

> And the twelve called together the whole community of the disciples and said, "It is not right that we should neglect the word of God in order to wait on tables. Therefore, friends, select from among yourselves seven men of good standing, full of the Spirit and of wisdom, whom we may appoint to this task, while we, for our part, will devote ourselves to prayer and to serving the word."
>
> Acts 6:2–4

In choosing the seven deacons the apostles expanded the breadth of leadership available to the community, empowered persons to join them in the task of ministry, and shared their own leadership with others, all done to meet the vision of what their ministry entailed, trusting the discernment of the community as a whole and the power of the Holy Spirit to raise up those competent and necessary for this vital ministry. Out of their willingness to share the new power they had received the apostles built an effective team that would expand the capabilities of the Christians and make new disciples.

Productive leaders follow the example of the apostles. They realize that the ministry of the church is larger than their own abilities to carry out all the responsibilities of that ministry and they seek out others to share in the work. Trusting the equipping grace of the Holy Spirit, they move away from the singular focus of their own perspective and the limited range of their own competencies and empower others to share in the ministry of the church. They value the leadership of those they empower, knowing that the combined ministry of the team they are building is greater than the sum of the individual competencies of its members. They willingly offer to others the opportunity to serve by delegating responsibilities to them, thus opening the door for more focus and dedication on their own part. Furthermore, effective leaders value opinions that differ from their own, knowing that challenging dialogue creates new strength; therefore, they intentionally recruit leaders who will be willing to enter into creative reflection with them. The end result is a more productive ministry that makes more disciples.

Productive leaders *foster a sense of intimacy* within the team they build and within the church as a whole. "Intimacy" implies a sense of closeness and compassion in relationships that creates bonds of connection, bonds which approach those of being a family together. Just as families share in the highs and lows of life, depending upon one another for strength, support and love, churches that develop this sense of intimacy are there for one another, responding to needs that arise, concerned about what happens in one another's lives, rejoicing together in times that are good and sharing the tears that come when times are bad. This sense of intimacy requires an investment in and responsibility for the welfare of one another and creates a clear sense of mutuality within the relationships that are formed. With intimacy comes familiarity and understanding, both of which foster trust between persons, and all of this enables productive leaders to build an effective team of leaders and empower them to use their best abilities in the fulfillment of the ministry of the church.

Productive leaders *find healthy balances, especially between values and needs.* In previous chapters, much has been presented about the tension between the values of the church and the needs of the community and the necessity of creating a collaborative approach to maintaining and utilizing this tension. Without question, effective leaders are skilled at maintaining this tension in a productive manner. They are competent in creating dialogue between the two poles that allows each to hear, assess the importance of, and appreciate the significance of the other, then to use this dialogue to move toward fulfillment of the church's vision by honoring each pole and using the combined assets and strengths to make disciples. Beyond this balance, however, is another reality: the tension created is a product of the mindset and priorities of the church and its leaders. In other words, the tension between values and needs is a tension that is made manifest in the longings of the leaders of the church. In the final analysis, competent leaders are skilled at balancing the vision of the church and its pursuit of ministry with the people who represent the church's values and seek to fulfill its ministry. Healthy, productive leadership, therefore, connects the kingdom and its ministry with the people and their needs.

In the final verse of the twelfth chapter of I Corinthians, Paul moves toward the importance of this balance. Having laid out a convincing case for the proper use of spiritual gifts and the need for cooperation and mutual respect, imaging the Church as the Body of Christ, he pens the words " . . . *I will show you a still more excellent way.*"[1] These words serve as the introduction to the thirteenth chapter, in which he describes and explores the qualities of love, ending the chapter by dramatically emphasizing that love is the greatest of all the gifts. Thus, the means by which the church is able to function in a synergistic relationship is through loving one another. The words he uses to describe this love are worth noting:

> Love is patient; love is kind; love is not envious or boastful or arrogant or rude. It does not insist on its own way; it is not irritable or resentful; it does not rejoice in wrongdoing, but rejoices in the truth. It bears all things, believes all things, hopes all things, endures all things.[2]

Productive leaders live out this image of love in their relationships and seek to promote it by making it the guiding principle in their efforts to lead others. They constantly strive for balance between values and needs, through living out qualities of love and keeping the people personally connected with the vision and mission of the church.

Referring to the conduct of church meetings as a task of leadership, Philip Anderson wrote:

1. I Corinthians 12:31b
2. I Corinthians 13:4–7

The content of a meeting includes all the words that are spoken and all the feelings that are felt.

. . .

A meeting needs to be concerned with both ideas and feelings. [3]

He goes on to describe these two components of a meeting as "*instrumental*," referring to the stated agenda for the meeting, and "*foundational*," the needs of the people present for the meeting.[4] In translating this idea to the greater arena of the church's ministry and the call to make disciples, the tension between values and needs may be represented as the tension between *foundation*, who we are and what we represent, and *function*, what we seek to do to make disciples.[5] Productive leaders *are competent in creating a balance between the foundational values of the church and its functional requirements*. Churches that are effective in making disciples have a propensity to attend to each of these in a high degree. Creating this balance is worthy of continued reflection.

The task of leadership requires a high degree of discernment. Productivity is enhanced when leaders discern the vision of the church as the collaboration between the foundational and the functional aspects of its ministry. On a grand scale, this means that the church is involved in outreach and mission in fulfillment of its function as well as nurture and care as the foundation of their identity. On a practical level, this means that productive leaders do not ignore or dismiss the needs of the people in order to fulfill the church's ministry, nor do they sacrifice ministry in order to cater to the needs of the members. Thus, effective leadership may be seen as a product of the extent to which these two are combined. Leaders tend toward one of four possibilities.

High Function/High Foundation. Leaders focus their attention equally on the mission of the church and the needs of the people. They understand that the church is an institution that is made of people and that it is the people that *are* the church's ministry. They use the values and strengths of individuals to fulfill this ministry, and the ministry of the church to give expression to and affirm the worth of those individuals. They are concerned

---

3. Anderson, *Church Meetings That Matter*, p.16.

4. Anderson, *Church Meetings That Matter*, p. 19.

5. Accepting the meaning of Anderson's term "*instrumental*," the term "*functional*" is used here to further define Anderson's meaning in terms of the ministry of the church or the church's activity.

that the church makes disciples and they seek to fulfill this calling while making sure that loving one another within the body is expressed and lived out in the relationships present. Meetings are warm gatherings that are characterized by a sense of energy and collaboration. The synergy created between functional and foundational creates productivity and a healthy church that is attractive and fulfilling to individuals.

High Function/Low Foundation. Leaders focus their attention on the ministry of the church and the maintenance of the institution while ignoring or dismissing the needs of the people. They are agenda driven. While they may have a clear sense of vision, that vision is driven by the external image of the church and the need to claim success through visible metrics. Leadership styles are often heavy-handed, with a "top-down" perspective, creating a "Leader/Follower" mindset. Meetings focus more on facts and figures, finances and facilities, and discussion is held to a minimum, with no room for divergent or ancillary ideas. The church is often perceived by others as an active church, but members find little support for their personal struggles.

Low Function/High Foundation. Leaders focus their attention on the members of the church, their needs, desires, and longings and view this as the primary purpose of the church. There is a low sense of vision for future ministry and the church tends to be focused inward. Activities, which may be ample, are directed toward enjoyment and pleasure and toward enhancing the lives of individuals within the congregation. Ministry agendas often get lost in caring for one another. Meetings are often random discussions, more focused on what is happening in the lives of the members than on making disciples. There is a high degree of personal care and little concern for the greater Kingdom of God. The ethos of the church often is characterized by a "closed family" feeling and a "country club" image.

Low Function/Low Foundation. Leadership is scarce or, sometimes, absent. Leaders tend to be long serving, usually because there is a lack of depth in potential or future leaders. There is no sense of vision for the church's future ministry and care for others is not expressed or exists only within small groups. Meetings are perfunctory with little or nothing to show in the way of productive outcomes and are poorly attended. It is not uncommon to find a high degree of conflict between the members and ambivalence reigns supreme. For fear of losing what little they have, members are reluctant to implement or even consider anything that would change the status quo. The church, as a whole, is in decline and there is little hope for the future.

Truly productive leaders are competent in creating a healthy balance between the foundational needs of the church's people and the functional aspects of the church's ministry. Furthermore, they recognize that their leadership is the key to this balance and are intentional about cultivating both ends of the tension, moving toward collaboration. The ability to do this is a product of maturity: the maturity of the leader as well as the maturity of the church. As the church and the leader mature together, they grow into a sense of connection in which the ministry of the church and the values of the people are integrated, forming a synergistic whole. It is for this reason that outside leaders struggle to perceive what the church truly needs, and new leadership has to work hard at winning the confidence of the people; it is not so much a lack of trust as it is the inability to enter into the real lives of the people and identify with their personal and spiritual values.

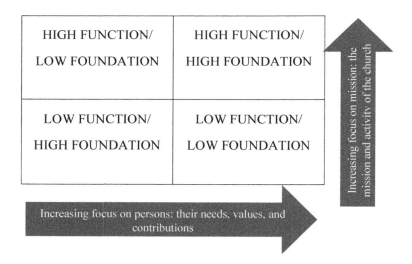

Growing in Competency

It is, therefore, important for leaders to regard their work as a collaborative effort and strive to grow in the competencies that make this possible. This can only happen by focusing attention on their individual skills and on the competencies of the people of the church at the same time. Productive churches have leaders that are willing to spend time growing leadership, knowing that a larger base of leaders will expand both the functional and foundational ministry of the church and enhance the abilities of those leaders already in place. They seek out and make available opportunities for growth and reflection and actively pursue ways in which they can continue to develop their own leadership skills and abilities. They are not afraid of evaluation and welcome critical reflection, knowing that, as the church works together to enhance these competencies, they mature into the high functioning productivity that God envisions for them.

For Continued Growth

a. Several instruments are available for assessing one's spiritual gifts, one of which is attached as Appendix C. Use this inventory to explore your personal gifts for ministry as you contemplate areas of growth for your own competencies. (This exercise may also be downloaded from the website *Productive Discipleship*: www.productivediscipleship.com)

b. The competencies of the church may be expressed as an integration of the foundational and functional aspects of leadership. Using the chart on page 116, asses the ministry of your church using the identifiers listed. Where would you rate the work of your church: High Function/High Foundation; High Function/Low Foundation; Low Function/High Foundation; Low Function/Low Foundation? Make a list of strategies that would improve that work and enable the church to move toward both higher function and higher foundation.

c. Repeat the above exercise with the aspects of your own leadership.

d. Use the chart in Appendix D to perform a self-evaluation of your own skills and competencies. (This chart may also be downloaded from the website *Productive Discipleship*: www.productivediscipleship.com)

10

Contributions of a Productive Leaders

Now in Joppa there was a disciple whose name was Tabitha, which in Greek is Dorcas. She was devoted to good works and acts of charity. At that time she became ill and died. When they had washed her, they laid her in a room upstairs. Since Lydda was near Joppa, the disciples, who heard that Peter was there, sent two men to him with the request, "Please come to us without delay." So Peter got up and went with them; and when he arrived, they took him to the room upstairs. All the widows stood beside him, weeping and showing tunics and other clothing that Dorcas had made while she was with them.

—ACTS 9:36–39

THE AUTHOR OF THE Book of Acts shares this story to validate and emphasize the role Peter played in the emerging church. Just as Jesus raised the young girl from her deathbed,[1] so Peter calls upon God to give Dorcas/Tabitha new life. Beyond this obvious meaning, however, is a powerful image of the natural reaction to death. Apparently, Peter did not know the woman, but was responding to the request of mutual friends. When he arrived at her home, those friends introduced Peter to Dorcas through the works of her hands: in those works, the apostle came to know her.

This story echoes what Jesus taught his disciples: *"You will know them by their fruits."*[2] In this teaching, he points out further that good trees don't produce bad fruit and bad trees don't produce good fruit. In other words, the fruit born by the tree is clear criteria for assessing the worth of the tree

1. Matthew 9:18–26
2. Matthew 7:16

itself. Therefore, our exploration of productive ministry ultimately leads us to a discussion of the works our hands and the fruit we bear: the contributions that result from our leadership. Indeed, the premise behind the entire content of this book is that leadership that does not produce good fruit for the kingdom of God is ineffective and falls short of the vision God has for the Church while productive leadership bears good fruit.

Perhaps one of the most profound voices speaking of the fruits of ministry is Lovett Weems, and his voice is worth hearing. In <u>Bearing Fruit</u>, he joins with Tom Berlin in saying that a recognition of contribution "... *may hold the most potential for revitalized church leadership*" and that the term "contribution" focuses on those characteristics of the leader as a steward of God's mission. They go on to describe the contribution of a fruitful congregation as including "... *experiencing God's presence, transforming lives, growing disciples, and serving others.*" The authors also point out that of the three categories of leadership identified by the Lewis Center (character, competency, contribution), it is this third category that is most neglected.[3]

Contribution and Productive Leadership

What does it truly mean to contribute to the ministry of the kingdom? What does it mean to bear fruit? Perhaps Weems is correct in identifying this arena of leadership as the least emphasized among clergy and judicatories. If so, then at least a part of the reason for the de-emphasis rests in the fact that it is an ambiguous topic that varies with individual leaders and their churches, one that is difficult to define and almost impossible to quantify. Unfortunately, "bearing fruit" is too easily expressed in the metric reporting of membership, attendance. and finances, since these are fairly easy to measure and form a graphic statement of the life of the church that can be tracked over time. Thus, the health of a church and the vitality of its ministry is often judged by how many people they have in worship, what increases in membership they have had over time and the growth in their financial stability. These are certainly good indicators of the growth of the church, but do they adequately indicate the growth of discipleship? They may indicate a church that is high functioning, but do they express the foundational contributions of leadership? The trap laid before leaders today is the ease with which they can measure the life of the church in terms of data and the difficulty they have in assessing the foundational ministry that

3. *Bearing Fruit*, p. xiii– xiv

truly makes disciples rather than members, givers, and attendees. For this reason, many church leaders and those who seek to guide them look past the qualities of leadership that evidence themselves in discipleship when they seek to measure effectiveness in the metrics of the church. However, effective, productive leaders see the fruit of their work in the transformed lives of people, which may, or may not, be represented in the statistics of the church.

How, then, is the contribution of productive leadership adequately expressed? This issue was addressed by the apostle Paul in his letter to the Galatians.[4]

> By contrast, the fruit of the Spirit is love, joy, peace, patience, kindness, generosity, faithfulness, gentleness, and self-control. There is no law against such things.

While the words that Paul wrote in these verses were an appeal to the Galatians to avoid the desires of the flesh and seek the work of the Spirit, they are expressed within the greater context of Paul's concern: the Law provides a superb measuring stick for judging righteous actions, but the true desire of God is a relationship that can only be measured in the righteousness of the heart, formed in response to the love expressed in Jesus Christ. The evidence of this relationship is indicated by the extent to which persons live lives characterized by the fruits of the Spirit, characteristics which also manifest themselves in productive leadership. The contribution of productive leaders, therefore, must be expressed in the qualities of leadership that bear the fruits of the Spirit, the foundational component of leadership, which then lead to the production of the measurable statistics of the church, being evidence of the effectiveness of the functional aspects of the church's ministry.

Contributions of Productive Leaders

Churches that are productive share common characteristics that are evidence of the fruits of the Spirit at work in their midst, fostered by productive leadership. The characteristics and competencies identified earlier empower the church to become a visible witness to the fruits of a leadership that makes disciples. While this witness is manifested in ways that are unique to each individual congregation, there are qualities of the church

---

4. Galatians 5:22–23

that are held in common among productive congregations and which become the goal and contribution of productive leadership, as observed by this author. These qualities reach beyond the program of the church—the activities in which the church engages—moving closer toward the nature of the church itself. That is, they must never be confused with a statement of what the church does in ministry, but who the church is. In this way, the work of productive leadership brings together the values and compassion of the church in a collaborative way to produce a new identity. The following is an expression of these qualities, articulated as the goals toward which productive leaders strive.

Productive leaders *strive for a church that honors its legacy and embraces its future.* Too often, churches find themselves living in their history and their ministry seeks to recapture or recreate the glory days of the past. Occasionally a church chooses to ignore what it was in order to become what it might be. Truly productive churches do neither of these. Productive leaders understand that both the traditional values of the church and the longings of the people are a part of who the church is and work to bring these together in the life and ministry of the church. There is a traditional saying that lies close to the heart of productive leaders and that expresses their perspective on the life of the church and the goals toward which they strive.

> *Yesterday has come and gone; tomorrow has not yet arrived. We have the memories of the past and hope of the future, but today is the only day that we are alive.*

These words express a perspective on life that lives in the "now." It neither dwells on the things that have been nor lives exclusively in a hope for things to be: it uses each of these to shape the current reality of one's existence, knowing that every past memory was and every future reality will be lived in a "now" moment. Jesus invited his disciples to consider the importance of living each moment with this perspective.

> *Consider the lilies of the field, how they grow; they neither toil nor spin, yet I tell you, even Solomon in all his glory was not clothed like one of these. But if God so clothes the grass of the field, which is alive today and tomorrow is thrown into the oven, will he not much more clothe you—you of little faith? . . . So do not worry about tomorrow, for tomorrow will bring worries of its own. Today's trouble is enough for today.*[5]

5. Matthew 6:28–34

Productive leaders strive to create a church and a ministry that is focused on the presence of God's Spirit, which is both a past and a future reality and which empowers them to live in the confidence of the past providence of God and the future promise of God's grace yet focuses on the moment of their ministry and life and claims the work of the Spirit to utilize each day to bear fruit and make disciples. There is a sense of liminality in productive leaders, a sense that every moment of their life and ministry is a defining moment that will forever shape who they are and what they do.

Productive leaders seek *a ministry that is both foundational and functional.* As explored in the previous chapter, one of the primary characteristics of healthy churches and productive leadership is the ability to integrate the work of the church with the needs of the people. This is more than the challenge of finding a balance between the two: balance rests on compromise; integration implies a relationship of synergy in which collaboration creates new realities that bring the best of both priorities to bear on the current life of the church. Thus, churches that manifest this characteristic are warm and loving inwardly while being aggressively involved in ministries and activities that seek to extend the kingdom of God. Words commonly used to describe these churches are "friendly," "welcoming," "invitational," "busy," "missional." Often, they are diverse in their makeup, but this diversity may manifest itself in many ways, including the age of the members, their socio-economic status or educational level, their political affiliations or their theological perspective. These churches and their leaders actively seek out and welcome this diversity, knowing that it produces strength and opens the doors to new possibilities in their life together. While they may exude a sense of harmony, it is not based on like-mindedness, but the clear understanding that disciples come in many forms and that God's love is not uniquely offered to any one set of opinions or values. Thus, productive leaders focus their attention on the people within their midst as the strength of the church and guide them to faithful expressions of their values in the pursuit of the kingdom and bearing fruit.

Productive leaders produce *a ministry that is focused on people.* The integration of the foundational and functional ministry of the church is not for the sake of fulfilling institutional mandates, but to fulfill the needs and longings of people in their midst. As important as institutional values are, productive leaders do not focus their attention on preserving these values, but on using them to shape the world in which they live, which means shaping the lives of the people with whom they have contact, both within the institution and outside of it. Commenting on the writing of Mary Parker Follett, an author from the early twentieth century who decried the promotion of personal honesty over issues of social justice, Lovett Weems states: *"Effective leadership begins not with some fixed ideology . . . Leadership begins with people."*[6] The contribution of productive leadership is not the preservation of the heritage of the church for future generations, but people whose lives are touched and transformed by the Holy Spirit, and the ministry that characterizes such contribution exudes the passion and compassion for people evidenced in the Gospels.

Productive leaders *seek to create a ministry that focuses beyond the walls of the church.* Productive churches evidence a healthy foundational ministry that lifts up the people of the church as an essential strength of its life, which is united with a strong functional ministry that turns outward and involves itself in the lives of the people of the community. Productive leaders understand that the gospel message contained in the scriptures of the New Testament was a message that begged to be proclaimed in the words and actions of the early disciples, who became apostles and set out to transform the world with this message. Thus, while certainly caring for those inside the institution of the church, productive leaders use the strength of these persons to thrust the transforming message of the gospel into the world, to reshape the lives of those outside the church and journey toward the greater kingdom of God. The struggle for outward movement is as old as the gospel itself and Jesus was not exempt from this struggle. He was often criticized by the pharisees for ignoring the dictates of the law, gathering with the poor and disenfranchised, eating with "sinners." In the early days of the Methodist movement, the same struggle was born in the relationship between John Wesley and George Whitfield.

In the early days of the Methodists, Whitfield, a student at Oxford, came under the influence of John and Charles Wesley and they became his mentors in the faith. He quickly rose to popularity because of his heartfelt, impassioned, and often fiery preaching, bringing hundreds to a new faith. It was a critical moment in history, both for the Methodist movement and for the Protestant revival, one that would prove life shaping, for the Wesleys, for Methodists in Great Britain, and, eventually for the westward expansion of Protestantism in the new world.

> *. . . at this critical phase of the revival, young, exuberant, Whitefield took the lead, dragging behind the older, more cautious Wesley. In*

---

6. Weems, *Leadership in the Wesleyan Spirit*, p.17.

> *spring 1739 Whitefield took the momentous step of preaching out-*
> *doors—first to the grimy coalminers around Bristol, and then to*
> *the street poor of London. This turned methodism outward, from*
> *respectable Anglican societies toward the huge unchurched mass.*
> *Whitefield now pushed the reluctant Wesleys into following him as*
> *field preachers.[7]*

Perhaps this one moment in history proved to be the most significant shift for the Methodists, moving them from the confines of the Church and the people therein to the needs of the world and transforming the movement into an evangelical exercise in reforming that world. Productive leaders seek to create a ministry with this same outward thrust and productive churches are characterized by the urgency of evangelism displayed by George Whitfield. They understand that discipleship is grown through the foundational ministry of the church, but disciples are made through outward reaching functional ministry.

Thus, logical thinking leads to understanding that productive leaders *make disciples.* Jesus spent the early days of his ministry teaching his disciples how to live their lives in a close and dependent relationship upon God, but the later days of that ministry were focused on instilling within his followers the desire to take the message they had learned to the remote towns and villages of their surroundings. The progression of Matthew's Gospel demonstrates this movement clearly. In the first public teaching that the author presents, Jesus invites his disciples to see God's blessings in the simple things of life and to live in a manner that reflects those blessings. The words of the "Beatitudes" and the teachings that follow (chapters 5-7 of Matthew) create a foundation for their faith that will lead to a simple life that manifests a love toward others through their relationships, both with God and with their neighbors. With his decision to journey to Jerusalem and the cross, however, this inward centered faith that shapes the spiritual lives of the disciples is refocused outwardly as Jesus begins to prepare them for their future life without him. His teachings shift from caring for themselves to responsibility for the kingdom of God (note the parables of the two sons and the wicked tenants in chapter 21). The final words spoken by Jesus in this gospel are

---

7. J.D. Walsh, "Wesley vs. Whitfield" *Christian History* Issue #38, 1993.

Go therefore and make disciples of all nations, baptizing them in the name of the Father and of the Son and of the Holy Spirit, and teaching them to obey everything that I have commanded you.[8]

As the extension of the ministry of Jesus, productive leaders use the strength of faith found in the disciples of the church to extend outward and make new disciples, understanding that the very purpose of discipleship is the growth of the kingdom of God. Inspired and motivated by God's vision for the church, they clearly see the calling of the congregation to draw others into the kingdom, toward the ultimate goal of ushering in the reign of God on earth. Thus, the coming kingdom is not only a future hope but the goal of all the work that they do in ministry, toward which they strive.

Productive leaders create *a ministry that has before it the vision of God's kingdom.* The underlying focus of this entire work has been that the Church, both local and universal, exists not for itself and its own edification, but for the promotion of the kingdom of God. Effectiveness in ministry is not measured by the size of buildings or the worth of financial holdings, nor by the rewards and accolades heaped upon it. The ultimate criteria for judging the effectiveness of ministry is the extent to which it has lived out the faith in its relationship to the people of the world. Based on the words of Matthew 6:33, the question we will be asked on the day of judgment is *"Have you strived for the kingdom of God above all things?"* Indeed, the teaching of these words convince us that if we can contribute this one thing, all else will follow and the ministry of the church will be productive. From the inception of their work, productive leaders envision the kingdom of God in their midst and move toward it in their planning, their implementation, and their evaluation of the ministry to which they give themselves. This vision forms the foundation for their values and shapes everything they do. Furthermore, this vision is not of what *might* happen at some point in the future, but of what *can* happen with the ministry of the church; not a hope that God will someday transform the world, but the commitment to being a part of God's transforming power in each moment of life. It is not given birth in a theological ideology, but in a deep and heartfelt sense of calling that connects individual leadership with the very Spirit of God at work in the world. They welcome the call of Jesus that invites them to cast their nets into deeper waters, knowing that going where God leads them brings blessing and fulfillment, not only in their own lives, but in the lives

8. Matthew 28:19-20

of others, and they find those blessings in the full nets of people, brought into the boat of God's kingdom as the new disciples.

11

The Emerging, Productive Church

But Peter, standing with the eleven, raised his voice and addressed them, "Men of Judea and all who live in Jerusalem, let this be known to you, and listen to what I say. Indeed, these are not drunk, as you suppose, for it is only nine o'clock in the morning. No, this is what was spoken through the prophet Joel:

'In the last days it will be, God declares,
that I will pour out my Spirit upon all flesh,
and your sons and your daughters shall prophesy,
and your young men shall see visions,
and your old men shall dream dreams.
Even upon my slaves, both men and women,
in those days I will pour out my Spirit;
and they shall prophesy.
And I will show portents in the heaven above
and signs on the earth below,
blood, and fire, and smoky mist.
The sun shall be turned to darkness
and the moon to blood,
before the coming of the Lord's great and glorious day.
Then everyone who calls on the name of the Lord shall be saved.'

—ACTS 2:14–21

IT WAS THE FESTIVAL of Pentecost, a day that would later come to be recognized as the birthday of the Church. The gift of the Holy Spirit that invaded the hearts of the Apostles would give rise to an institution that would reshape the world and change the lives of millions of people, for thousands of generations. The events of that day would eventually result in laws, ethical standards, monarchies, and dynasties, providing spiritual and moral direction to people and nations for over two millennia. We, those who are shaping and reading the words of this book, are the product of the events of that day. Did Peter know all these things? Surely not! His limited perspective of the physical and political world could not provide the insight into what God would bring forth that was necessary for such vision. But Peter did know one thing, the most important thing: God was at work, and God would use the twelve apostles to bring into reality the Church that God envisioned. Peter did not have to see clearly into the future; he only had to trust the leading presence of God in the moment.

In the years, decades, and generations to come, what will the Church look like? What will our local church look like? Many have speculated on the answers to these questions. Some forecasts are hopeful, while others are filled with despair. Some see global growth and expansion; others see decline and demise. Many look forward in hope, expecting the Church to reshape the world into a humane and compassionate place to live; others dismiss the standards of the Church as archaic and out-of-touch with reality.

As I write these words, the United States, indeed, the whole world, is in the midst of the now infamous Covid-19 pandemic. The deathly spread of this virus has forced everyone into patterns of behavior that they could neither expect nor imagine. Homes have suddenly become offices, schoolrooms, and, in some cases, prison-like environments as people seek to protect themselves and others from the spread of this disease. Social gatherings are relegated to online chats, meetings have become virtual, and facemasks are daily attire. What was originally seen as a minor diversion from the status quo has turned into a year-long ordeal that is devastating lives, bringing rampant unemployment and sending the world economy into a tailspin: who knows what the long-term changes will be when the world finally recovers? At this point, no-one knows what the future will bring; yet everyone knows that it will not look like the past and we will all be driven into a new normal.

The Church, too, has been altered by the pandemic. Only a few months ago I argued that "on-line" church was an oxymoron that defied the very meaning of the word: "Ecclesia," the Greek word that translates to "church," means *the people gathered.* How can you have "church" with-out the people being together? Now I find myself standing in an empty sanctuary on Sunday morning, preaching to a camera and struggling to connect the members of my church with God and with one another as they sit in their homes, physically distanced from one another yet spiritually connected, and I have learned that there are many ways to "gather" that go beyond physical proximity. All of us serving churches have been compelled to find a new way of being in ministry, and from our efforts have come some amazing programs and accompanying revelations. At our church, we have discovered that our on-line presence in worship more than doubled our average attendance, with worshippers joining us from other communi-ties, states, and even nations. While incredibly involved in missions to our local community, none of us could see a time when we would be actively and intimately bound to Christians in India on a weekly, almost daily, basis, but out of the crisis of isolation the Spirit has brought connection.

In his book The Gospel According to Peanuts, Robert Short talks about "Divine Imagination." Looking into the clouds, Charlie Brown finds himself rather short-sighted in the presence of the vivid imagination of his best friend Linus. Short connects the visionary perspective of Linus to a church that sees itself in the broader context of life—all of life—and quotes Karl Barth as saying that it is " . . . *the ability to see sermons in stones and good in everything.*" Short goes on to say that if the Church fails to use its divine imagination, it will find itself like Charlie Brown, embarrassed by a world far more capable of vision and creativity.[1] As the Holy Spirit fell upon Peter and the apostles, a new imagination arose, breaking them out of the small world of a band of disciples following a would-be messiah into the apostles, sent into the world with a life changing, world altering mes-sage. It is this divine imagination that lies at the heart of the productive church, a church that is able to see God's vision beyond the reality of the present moment, to hear God's voice above the din of human striving, and to shape their present reality in the hope of what will come. It is in this Divine Imagination that the future of the Church lies, and the enduring local church will learn how to exercise and utilize their divine imagination. While we cannot predict the exact shape of this yet-to-emerge church, we can see some attributes that it will have.

That church will be *provisional,* understanding that the life of the church is not a permanent fixture, but a transient instrument of service to

1. Short *The Gospel According to Peanuts* pp. 32–33.

the kingdom. Consider the image of a rock climber. That person begins with a firm handhold, gripped tenaciously to provide security on the face of the rock. This hold is then followed by the other hand, then the feet, all placed in the most advantageous locations to allow the climber to be connected to the side of the cliff. Once firmly located, however, the climber must let go to reach for a higher hold or else forever remain affixed to the face of the rock. Thus, rock climbing becomes a continuous process of grabbing hold and letting go, utilizing the most advantageous outcroppings and crevices to find a place to stand in the moment while reaching upward for that next opportunity for a grip that will allow progress, ever moving toward the ultimate goal of the summit. The emerging church will hold tightly to those attributes of the church that make disciples in the current moment of its life but will always be looking toward the future and how they can best serve the greater kingdom of God, always climbing toward that kingdom. When new opportunities present themselves, the people of this church will be willing to let go of the old, knowing that it served its purpose, and reach out for the new, prepared and committed to the prospects that it presents. Thus, the productive church that emerges will live with a sense of tentativeness, in the most positive sense of that word, that commits itself to the goal and not the program, to the need to grow and develop so that they may serve the future needs of the community in which they are located.

That church will be *people oriented*. As a "baby boomer" I grew up in an era when the Church was rapidly expanding. New congregations of every denomination were emerging in metropolitan areas and church architecture exploded in a variety of styles. Some embellished the classic gothic style, some sought to enhance the look of the pioneering spirit of the nineteenth century, still others ignored past designs and developed an entirely new look that reflected the new, emerging theology of the era. The church in which I was raised was originally built in a style that sought to blend the past with the future, with a quite traditional chancel and an elevated choir loft, but a knave absent of pews, using folding chairs instead. A church viewed as on the "cutting edge" of the new and emerging wave of growth, it became a model for other new churches. After fifteen years, however, the church council proposed building a new sanctuary, with a movable pulpit and a flexible space that would be open to a variety of configurations, seeking to reflect a change in their theological perspective that shifted the focus away from the chancel and the preacher and onto the community of faith. Once again, it was on the cutting edge of the emerging church and the trend became that of rethinking the meaning of "church." The new wave of theology called for churches to move outside their four cozy walls and for the members of congregations to focus on the needs of the people rather than the shape of building and its worship space. Yet over fifty years later, we are still enamored with the beauty of our buildings and the comfort that they provide, often to the exclusion of the suffering people who live in our neighborhoods. In all of the churches with whom I have worked, the annual budget for building and maintenance is considerably larger than the amount spent for mission and outreach. In times of financial strain, which items get reduced first? Almost always budget cuts begin with program and staff, justified with words like *We have to keep the building up so we can do ministry.* Often these cuts begin a downward spiral and indicate that the church has transitioned into the declining trend of their lifeline. The emerging productive church will realize that its true identity rests in neither a building nor a location, but in the congregation. They will seek to empower the people of their church to be involved in making disciples beyond the walls of the building. The sanctuary and classrooms will shift from being mere havens of comfort and social involvement and become training grounds that motivate and energize members of the congregation to involve themselves in the needs of the people of their community and the world. To do this, the church will shift its focus from the form of its ministry to the function of it, away from the "how" and onto the "why" as they find new and creative ways to be the church.

Therefore, that church will *focus on mission.* The wave of growth and rapid expansion experienced by the Protestant Church in the middle of the twentieth century, that time when many of our small churches began to thrive, was fueled by a spirit of revival. We believed that if you could get the people to realize that Jesus was the solution to their problems and that following him would bring the reward of heaven, then we had fulfilled the purpose of the church. The fruit borne from this focus created large numbers of people in the pews, but often fell short of making disciples. People came to and maintained their relationship with the church in order to fulfill needs and desires in their own lives, primarily the need for community and a sense of belonging. While those needs still exist in today's world, they have been eclipsed by a desire to make a difference. Our current generation is more focused on causes than institutions. Local churches struggle to meet budgets, but a "go-fund-me" page for a family in crisis will raise thousands of dollars over a matter of days. People respond more quickly to real, concrete needs than to maintenance and salaries. People want to make a difference and they want to see the difference they make. Leaders in the emerging church will learn to be transparent in the church's ministry in a manner that makes the needs of others visible and envisions a new world for them through the work of the church, then celebrates the successes that materialize. Yet, while focused on mission, the church will not neglect caring for one another and the values they hold dear. Instead, it will use the care extended as a means by which they can motivate and empower persons to use their values in order to be productive.

The emerging church will be more *diverse*. As the focus of the church moves toward mission, people will come to the church because of what it does rather than who it is. Rather than seeking a homogeneity of desires and values, the church will find its meaning in the strengths people bring to the church; rather than their conformity to certain images of what the church is supposed to be, the church will honor persons for who they are. As true diversity emerges, the church will discover a shift away from conflict and confrontation toward a spirit of collaboration, seeking out different opinions, ideas, and strengths in ministry as a means of enhancing the productivity of the church. Leaders will become managers, employing the strengths present in the diverse members and deploying persons in the most effective way to use those strengths.

That church will also be more *efficient*. Focus on fewer programs and higher benefit will lead to what Brandon O'Brien calls a "high accountability/low control" ministry.[2] Less time will be spent on the formalities and protocols of meetings and more time spent on equipping persons for ministry. The classroom will become a training ground for persons to explore how to live out the kingdom of God in the midst of the world and it's issues, and sermons will motivate people to move toward making disciples rather than building churches and raising budgets. Less time will be spent on deciding what to do and how to do it and more time spent on engaging in acts of mercy and grace, diminishing the need for more meetings and changing the nature of those meetings away from giving reports and toward celebrating progress. There will be fewer officers in the church yet more leaders as the emphasis shifts from high profile, controlling personalities toward servant leadership. Thus, the energy of the church will be focused on making disciples rather than on creating programs.

2. O'Brien *The Strategically Small Church*, ch. 5.

Finally, that church will become productive. Complacency will be replaced by activity as the church's vision brings a sense of hope for the church and its future and the people rediscover the meaning of community and mission. They will begin to sense a new purpose in their faith that connects them with a reality that exists beyond their current circumstances and present moment of time. All of the above characteristics of the emerging church combined will move it toward its vision of the kingdom of God on earth.

Appendix A

Discerning the Vision

Phase 1—Facing Reality: Recognizing Who We Are

A.

Assess the current values of your church:

1. Utilize current and past demographics to recognize patterns in the church's history.
2. Note traditions of the church and what they represent, including ongoing programs and ministries.
3. Invite members and leaders to complete the statement: *"I joined the church because ... "* Use this information to summarize what in the values of the church are attractive.

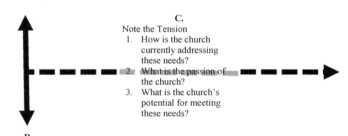

C.

Note the Tension

1. How is the church currently addressing these needs?
2. What is the passion of the church?
3. What is the church's potential for meeting these needs?

B.

Assess the current needs of your community:

1. Utilize current and past demographics to recognize patterns in the community's history and develop a profile of the community.
2. Visit with community leaders to determine projected trends in demographics, including population growth, economics, education and recreation.
3. Using the above information, note the positive and negative aspects of your community: the positive are your strengths; the negative represent opportunities for ministry.

Phase 2—Listening to God: Looking for More

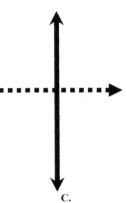

B.
Explore the values of the
church in light of the
scriptures:
- *Are the values of our
  church consistent with
  those found in these
  scriptures?*

A.
Engage the Scriptures:
1. Dedicate time to study the scriptures
   together.
2. Ask vital questions of the text(s) under
   study
   a. *What is the nature of discipleship
   revealed in this passage?*
   b. *When disciples are faithful to this
   revelation, what is the outcome that God
   brings?*
   c. *What is the fruit born for the Kingdom?*
   d. *What is revealed about the nature of the
   Kingdom of God?*

C.
Explore the needs of the
community in light of the
scriptures:
- *Are the needs of our
  community reflected in
  these scriptures?*

Phase 3—Moving Toward the Future: A New Vision

B.
Envision your church:
a. *If our church lived out the
   meaning of this passage,
   what would it look like?*
b. *What would have to change?*
c. *What resources do we have
   available that would enable
   us to become this church?*

A.
Apply the Scriptures:
*Reflect on the future
life of the church.*

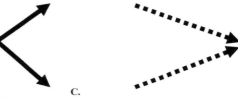

C.
Envision your ministry
a. *What ministries are, or might
   be, implied in the nature of
   discipleship revealed here?*
b. *If we chose to do this as a
   church, what resources do
   we have available that would
   prove helpful?*
c. *What fruit would we bear?*

Phase 4—Defining the Vision

a. *What is God seeking to accomplish through our church?*
b. *What can we do that would serve God's purpose?*
c. *What are the values held by our congregation that will enable us to accomplish this?*
d. *When accomplished, what will the church look like?*

■ ■ ■ ▶

■ ■ ■ ▶

God is calling

_____ *church*

to

_____

so that it can become

_____

_____

Appendix B

Characteristics of a Productive Leader

Use the list below to help determine your leadership characteristics. Using the identifying marks listed with each characteristic, determine the extent to which you see evidence of it using this scale:

1. This is not a characteristic I have

2. I seldom display this characteristic

3. This is a characteristic I can develop further

4. I am confident this is one of my characteristics

5. This characteristic is a strength in my leadership

Characteristic	1	2	3	4	5
Essential Characteristics					
Spiritual: is constantly aware of the presence of God's spirit and seeks God's guidance in all matters of decision making and action.					
Visionary: sees the potential and possibilities of the future and uses this vision as a source of guidance in leadership					
Servant: finds fulfillment in taking care of the needs of others and does not seek recognition in it					
Disciple: honors and recognizes the authority of others; willing to follow the leadership others provide					

Characteristic	1	2	3	4	5
Committed: dedicated to the church's vision and willing to work through obstacles to the fulfillment of that vision					
Passionate: fervent about the life and ministry of the church and willing to tell the church's story					
Compassionate: aware of the suffering of others and works to alleviate that suffering					
Authentic: lives a well-integrated life of faith and practice, belief and action; honest and worthy of trust					
Humble: seeks honor and recognition for the church and it's ministry, but not for oneself					

Functional Characteristics

Curious: Eager to learn and explore new concepts and ideas					
Active Listener: enters into conversations in order to understand what others are saying rather than present a singular point of view					
Self-assured: exudes a sense of trust and confidence without being arrogant					
Courageous: willing to step forward in a time of need; exudes a sense of boldness in new endeavors					
Tenacious: displays a sense of hopefulness in the face of difficulty; does not falter in their commitments					
Flexible: willing to adjust their attitudes and understanding in light of new possibilities					

Having noted these characteristics, determine:

- Which characteristics did you rate as a 4-5? These are your strengths: what are you doing to use these strengths in your leadership?

- Which characteristics did you rate as a 2-3? These are your potential strengths: make a list of positive changes that you could make to improve your use of these characteristics and create strategies to put these changes in place.

- What characteristics do you seem to lack in your leadership (rated 1)? How can you compensate for this lack?

As an added benefit, invite others to complete this inventory on your behalf, assessing your leadership characteristics as they perceive you. Compare your responses and allow the added perspective to initiate a conversation about your leadership strengths. Use the information and insight gained to develop a plan for utilizing your inherent strengths and strengthening your leadership in areas that have potential.

It might also be helpful to invite the leadership team of your church to complete this inventory on themselves. Sharing conversation about the inherent characteristics of your team can be beneficial in assigning tasks, planning ministries and developing future leaders.

Appendix C

Inventory of Spiritual Gifts

In the following table, six situations are presented that are typical of life and ministry in the church. Read each one and consider your response or action that would be typical of your leadership. Consider which of the listed responses allows you to feel most comfortable and place an "x" in the appropriate column (you may be comfortable with more than one response, so feel free to mark more than one). To assist your assessment, think of an actual instance or event and remember how you felt, how you acted or how you responded to the situation. *Remember, this is an inventory, not a test . . . there are no right or wrong answers.*

When you have reviewed and responded to all six circumstances, add the total number of responses in each column and write that total in the final row. For instance, if you marked an "x" in column 1 for four of the settings, your total for that column will be 4.

After completing the totals, read the accompanying information as a means of identifying your spiritual gifts.

	1	2	3	4	5	6	7

A. In a meeting, I am happy to:

1. Share what I think God is leading us to do
2. Make sure everyone has the right materials
3. Help the people understand the topic better
4. Encourage the people to make a positive response
5. Offer financial support to aid the ministry
6. Volunteer my time to help others
7. See to it that everyone is included

B. In a study group, I am the one who:

1. Reminds the people of God's vision
2. Makes sure the room is properly set and comfortable
3. Likes to share my opinions and ideas
4. Suggests ways we can live out the lesson
5. Makes an appeal for special projects
6. Helps the class accept mission opportunities
7. Calls people when they are absent

C. At social gatherings, I like to:

1. Remind people what it means to be the Church
2. Serve the food and drinks
3. Lead the people in games and activities
4. Encourage others to share in the activities and conversation
5. Provide the refreshments
6. Make sure everyone has what they need
7. See to it that no-one is left out

	1	2	3	4	5	6	7

D. When telling others about the church, I am most proud about how we:

1. Are doing God's will
2. Are involved in mission projects
3. Have a wonderful education program
4. Lead people to faith
5. Are generous and financially stable
6. Are willing to tackle virtually any project that is worthwhile
7. Include everyone in the church family

E. I can help the church most by:

1. Leading the people to embrace God's vision for us
2. Volunteering to help around the church
3. Teaching different classes
4. Encouraging people to get involved
5. Giving money to further its ministries
6. Taking care of other members
7. Raising its awareness of the needs of others

F. To me, the greatest need is for the church to:

1. Listen to God and follow God's will
2. Make sure that the building is clean and comfortable
3. Have a great education program
4. Lead everyone to a strong commitment
5. Be financially secure
6. Take care of others
7. Be an advocate for the less fortunate people of the world

Total

In the twelfth chapter of Romans, Paul identifies seven spiritual gifts, to which he calls the church's attention. There are additional gifts listed in some of the other books in the New Testament, including I Corinthians (12:1-27), Ephesians (4:1-7) and I Peter (4:8-11). You may want to take a look at some of these other gifts, too. All in all, there are over 30 spiritual gifts listed in the New Testament. However, our attention focuses on these seven as we consider our competencies for ministry. These seven gifts may be defined as follows.

1. **Prophecy**—The ability to discern God's will and vision and the willingness to make that vision known to others. One who has the gift of prophecy has a close spiritual connection with God evidenced by an active prayer life and is able to speak with a sense of authority to communicate his or her understanding of God's will and purpose.

2. **Service**—The willingness to engage in detailed tasks that enable the church to function smoothly. People who serve pay attention to details, are willing to invest their time and talents for the sake of others, and seldom want credit for what they do.

3. **Teaching**—Those who teach like to invest themselves in the lives of others, sharing their wisdom and understanding in order to help them grow closer to God. They have a deep and growing faith and are always willing to explore new ideas as they move closer to God.

4. **Exhortation**—People with this gift are encouragers, who enjoy helping others make deeper commitments in faith. They are generally "people-persons" who take the faith and spiritual wellbeing of others very seriously.

5. **Contributing**—Those with this gift are generous with their personal and financial resources and enjoy seeing their contributions make a difference in the life and ministry of the church. They understand how financial stewardship is a necessity in the life and health of the church and set an example for others to follow.

6. **Helping**—This is the gift of making sure that others have what they need. Helpers lead with their hearts, seeing what they can do to make life better for their friends and for other members of the church family. Through helping, these persons affirm the value of others.

7. **Mercy**—The gift of mercy is also a gift of compassion, feeling the pain of others. Those with this gift can often be found in hospitals, visiting shut-ins and taking care of those who have been beaten down by life. They lead the church to be aware of the needs of others and to be involved in solving the problems that cause pain, oppression and injustice.

As you consider these seven spiritual gifts, remember the inventory you just took and the total responses for each of the seven columns. Match your highest scores with the number of the gifts listed above and circle the number of the gift (or gifts) that are indicated by your responses. This could be your God-given gift (or gifts) for ministry. You may agree with the indication and already know that God has given you this gift, or you may be surprised by what you have just discovered. In considering your own competencies for ministry, you would do well to explore your gifts further and make a plan for how you can strengthen it in your ministry and become better able to use it for the fulfillment of your calling

Appendix D

Assessing Skills and Competencies

Use the list below to determine the extent to which you utilize competencies inherent in productive leaders. Rate your use of the competency using this scale:

1. This is not a competency I have

2. I am not comfortable using this competency

3. This is a competency I need to work on

4. I am comfortable using this competency

5. This competency is a strength in my leadership

	1	2	3	4	5
Guided by the church's vision					
Makes the vision a priority in decision making					
References the vision often in discussions					
Shares the vision openly with non-members					
Understands leadership as a dynamic process					
Welcomes new ideas					
Places ministry of the church above own desires					
Consistently monitors and evaluates leadership style					

	1	2	3	4	5
Understands and appreciates the culture of the church					
Knows the history of the church					
References past leadership with respect					
Celebrates the saints of the church					
Willingly shares power and responsibility					
Invites open discussion of issues					
Seeks out opinions from others					
Willingly delegates responsibilities					
Supports the work of others by providing resources					
Ensures that proper meeting notes are maintained					
Anticipates information needed for decision making					
Creates and shares agendas in advance					
Communicates clearly, consistently and effectively					
Has a system for informing other leaders of upcoming issues					
Initiates conversations regarding the ministry of the church					
Shares information from meetings with absentees					
Honors the work of others					
Publicly recognizes the work of leaders					
Expresses gratitude to others for their work					
Relates accomplishments to the church's vision					
Works to build an effective team					
Actively seeks others to work in the ministry of the church					
Provides means for others to grow in leadership					
Willingly works with people of differing opinions					

	1	2	3	4	5
Fosters a sense of intimacy					
Regularly inquires about the needs of other leaders					
Includes a time of personal care as a part of meeting agendas					
Celebrates with other leaders in the important moments of their lives					

Having noted these competencies, determine:

- Which competencies did you rate as a 4-5? These are your strengths: what are you doing to use these strengths in your leadership?

- Which competencies did you rate as a 2-3? These are your potential strengths: make a list of positive changes that you could make to improve your use of these characteristics and create strategies to put these changes in place.

- What competencies do you seem to lack in your leadership (rated 1)? How can you compensate for this lack?

As an added benefit, invite others to complete this inventory on your behalf, assessing your competencies as they perceive you. Compare your responses and allow the added perspective to initiate a conversation about your leadership strengths. Use the information and insight gained to develop a plan for utilizing your inherent strengths and strengthening your leadership in areas that have potential.

It might also be helpful to invite the leadership team of your church to complete this inventory on themselves. Sharing conversation about the inherent characteristics of your team can be beneficial in assigning tasks, planning ministries and developing future leaders.

Appendix E

Additional Resources

In order for churches to make an honest and accurate assessment of their community and its needs, they must access this information from outside sources. A healthy relationship with the leaders of the community can provide significant resources for this assessment, especially in terms of growth trends, future development and community priorities. Therefore, a valuable resource for study rests in the mayor, city manager, Chamber of Commerce director and school superintendent. In addition to these, much information is available online that can provide national, regional and local trends in population growth and there are several research institutes that assess this information in light of religious trends. Listed here are a few of those that have been used by this author. In addition, many denominations and judicatories have their own resource tools/boards that make information available to local churches.

- The Association of Religion Data Archives (www.theARDA.com) *is a compendium of information gathered by various religious researchers that can access local and regional information by zip code*

- Barna (https://www.barna.com/) *provides accurate information about culture and religious trends, along with insightful analysis that may provide help in developing ministries*

- Mission Insight (https://missioninsite.com/) *provides comprehensive, up-to-date information about religious values and preferences and is customizable for defining specific parish areas*

- United States Census Bureau (https://www.census.gov/) *provides information on a national scale and is especially helpful in showing/predicting national trends*

Bibliography

Anderson, Philip A. *Church Meetings That Matter*. New York: Pilgrim, 1965.

Arndt, William F. and Gingrich, F. Wilbur, *A Greek-English Lexicon of the New Testament*. Chicago: University of Chicago Press, 1957.

Callahan, Kennon L., *Twelve Keys to an Effective Church*. San Francisco: Jossey-Bass, 2010.

Follet, Mary Parker. *The New State*. New York: Longman, Green and Company. 1923

Keating, Charles J. *The Leadership Book*. New York: Paulist, 1982.

Leadership Defined: In Depth Interviews with America's Top Leadership Experts. (Interviews conducted by David E. Wright) Sevierville, Tennessee: Insight, 2005.

McNeal, Reggie. *Missional Renaissance*. San Francisco: Jossey-Bass, 2009.

O'Brien, Brandon J. *The Strategically Small Church*. Minneapolis: Bethany House, 2010.

Outler, Albert C., ed. *John Wesley*. New York: Oxford University Press, 1964.

Short, Robert L. *The Gospel According to Peanuts*. Richmond: John Knox, 1964.

Walsh, J.D. "Wesley vs. Whitfield" *Christian History* #38. Worcester, PA: Christian History Institute, 1993.

Weems, Lovett H. *Church Leadership*. Nashville, Abingdon, 2010.

Weems, Lovett H. *Leadership in the Wesleyan Spirit*. Nashville: Abingdon, 1999.

Weems, Lovett H. and Berlin, Tom. *Bearing Fruit*. Nashville: Abingdon, 2011

White, James F. *A Brief History of Christian Worship*. Nashville: Abingdon,1993.

Made in the USA
Middletown, DE
23 March 2022